SYSTEMATIC PROGRAMMING
An Introduction

Prentice-Hall
Series in Automatic Computation

George E. Forsythe, editor

MARTIN, *Programming Real-Time Computing Systems*
MARTIN, *Systems Analysis for Data Transmission*
MARTIN, *Telecommunications and the Computer*
MARTIN, *Teleprocessing Network Organization*
MARTIN AND NORMAN, *The Computerized Society*
MATHISON AND WALKER, *Computers and Telecommunications: Issues in Public Policy*
MCKEEMAN, et al., *A Compiler Generator*
MINSKY, *Computation: Finite and Infinite Machines*
MOORE, *Interval Analysis*
PLANE AND MCMILLAN, *Discrete Optimization:*
    Integer Programming and Network Analysis for Management Decisions
PRITSKER AND KIVIAT, *Simulation with GASP II:*
    a FORTRAN-Based Simulation Language
PYLYSHYN, editor, *Perspectives on the Computer Revolution*
RICH, *Internal Sorting Methods: Illustrated with PL/I Programs*
RUSTIN, editor, *Computer Networks*
RUSTIN, editor, *Debugging Techniques in Large Systems*
RUSTIN, editor, *Formal Semantics of Programming Languages*
SACKMAN AND CITRENBAUM, editors, *Online Planning: Towards Creative Problem-Solving*
SALTON, editor, *The SMART Retrieval System:*
    Experiments in Automatic Document Processing
SAMMET, *Programming Languages: History and Fundamentals*
SCHULTZ, *Digital Processing: A System Orientation*
SCHWARZ, et al., *Numerical Analysis of Symmetric Matrices*
SHERMAN, *Techniques in Computer Programming*
SIMON AND SIKLOSSY, editors, *Representation and Meaning: Experiments with*
    Information Processing Systems
SYNDER, *Chebyshev Methods in Numerical Approximation*
STERLING AND POLLACK, *Introduction to Statistical Data Processing*
STOUTMEYER, *PL/I Programming for Engineering and Science*
STROUD, *Approximate Calculation of Multiple Integrals*
STROUD AND SECREST, *Gaussian Quadrature Formulas*
TAVISS, editor, *The Computer Impact*
TRAUB, *Iterative Methods for the Solution of Polynomial Equations*
VAN TASSEL, *Computer Security Management*
VARGA, *Matrix Iterative Analysis*
VAZSONYI, *Problem Solving by Digital Computers with PL/I Programming*
WAITE, *Implementing Software for Non-Numeric Application*
WILKINSON, *Rounding Errors in Algebraic Processes*
ZIEGLER, *Time-Sharing Data Processing Systems*

SYSTEMATIC PROGRAMMING
An Introduction

NIKLAUS WIRTH

Eidgenössische Technische Hochschule
Zürich, Switzerland

PRENTICE-HALL, INC.

ENGLEWOOD CLIFFS, NEW JERSEY

Library of Congress Cataloging in Publication Data

WIRTH, NIKLAUS
  Systematic programming

(Prentice-Hall series in automatic computation)
    1. Electronic digital computers—Programming
    I. Title
    QA76.6.W5713   001.6'42   73-567824'
    ISBN 0-13-880369-2

10 9

Printed in the United States of America

PRENTICE-HALL INTERNATIONAL, INC., *London*
PRENTICE-HALL OF AUSTRALIA, PTY., LTD., *Sydney*
PRENTICE-HALL OF CANADA, LTD., *Toronto*
PRENTICE-HALL OF INDIA PRIVATE LIMITED, *New Delhi*
PRENTICE-HALL OF JAPAN, INC., *Tokyo*

Dedicated to the memory of
George E. Forsythe

CONTENTS

"All ... new systems of notation are such that one can accomplish nothing by means of them which would not also be accomplished without them; but the advantage is that when such a system of notation corresponds to the innermost essence of frequently occurring needs, one can solve the problems belonging in that category, indeed can mechanically solve them in cases so complicated that without such an aid even the genius becomes powerless. Thus it is with the invention of calculating by letters in general; thus it was with the differential calculus. . . .*

"It is the character of modern mathematics that through our language of signs and nomenclature, we possess a lever by which the most complicated arguments can be reduced to a particular mechanism. Science has thus gained an almost infinite richness, beauty, and solidity. But, in the day-to-day use of this tool, science has lost almost as much as it has gained. How often is that lever applied only mechanically, although the authorization for it generally implies certain tacit hypotheses. I demand that in *every* use of a system of notation and in *every* use of a particular concept, each user be conscious of the original conditions and *never* regard as his property any products of the mechanism beyond its clear authorization."

* From the letters of C. F. Gauss to Schumacher of May 15, 1843 and September 1, 1850.

PREFACE

My primary motivation is to introduce programming as the art or technique of constructing and formulating algorithms in a systematic manner, recognizing that it is a discipline in its own right. Algorithms, in the most general sense, are recipes for classes of data processing and control processes. They must be conceived as solid structures consisting of logically, reliably, and suitably designed building blocks.

The student should be educated to proceed methodically and systematically in the design of algorithms through the demonstration of problems and techniques that are typical of programming but independent of the area of application. For this reason, no specific area of application is emphasized as an end in itself; exercises and examples have been selected as demonstrations of generally valid problems and methods of solution. In the same spirit, the notation or programming language is deemphasized; the language is our tool but not an end in itself. The primary aim of programming courses should not be to teach perfection in the knowledge and use of all features and idiosyncrasies of a specific language. Rather, the language should mirror the fundamental and most important concepts of algorithms in an obvious, natural, and easily understandable way. It should also take into account the inherent properties and limitations of digital computers.

With due respect to the problem of program reliability, I have also tried to incorporate the basic ideas and techniques of program verification. After all, the aim in programming is to formulate entire classes of computational processes as algorithms. A conscientious designer, however, must be able to demonstrate that his product performs according to its specifications under all possible circumstances. But the commonly used methods of program testing (debugging) investigate only individual computations and not the entire class of computations that can be performed by the program under "scrutiny." To make generally valid assertions about the program itself, an analytic verification technique is indispensable.

The treatment of elementary verification methods necessitates an ability for abstraction on the part of the student to a somewhat higher degree than is usual in programming courses. Some reservations about the wisdom of including this topic in an elementary textbook have therefore been made. But I have come to the firm conviction that the basic concepts treated in this book—a restriction to the ideas of assertions and invariants—are of such fundamental significance that they belong in no other part of a curriculum other than in its very beginning. I also oppose the argument that this topic should be reserved for the more theoretically minded—program reliability is important in practice, not in theory. The concepts of program verification are actually the cornerstone for any deeper understanding of algorithms without which the programmer would have no other tool besides his own insufficient intuition.

This text is tailored to the people who view a course in the systematic construction of algorithms as part of their basic mathematical training rather than to those who wish to be able to occasionally encode a problem and then hand it to their computer for an instant solution.

The programming language ALGOL 60 is the basis for the notation employed throughout this textbook. But I have not used a literal adoption of ALGOL 60 because nowadays the computer—and with it programming—have a much wider area of application than 12 years ago, and an introduction to programming should not be exclusively oriented to one area of application. ALGOL 60 was designed primarily for numerical mathematics. Consequently, it allows the formulation of programs for other areas of application, where different structuring principles may be more appropriate and where other concepts dominate, often only by twisting and misusing the language. But the use of tools for purposes for which they were not intended should always be avoided in teaching and should certainly not be praised as an example worth imitating.

My strong desire to teach using a notation in which structures of processes and data emerge clearly and systematically rests on the observation that most people stick forever to the language that they first learned. This tendency is due not only to the oft-quoted inertia of the human mind but also to the fact that the "first" language represents a convenient framework through which abstract thought may obtain concrete form. With the first language, one not only acquires a vocabulary and a set of grammatical rules, but one also opens the gates to a new realm of thought. The choice of this language should therefore be made judiciously. It is a pity that the most widely used computer languages meet the requirements of logical and systematic teaching so poorly.

The prerequisites for this course are elementary mathematics. In particular, the student is expected to be familiar with the elements of propositional logic and the notion of mathematical induction. Familiarity with calculus is hardly necessary—except for some examples and exercises that could be skipped.

It is important that the student actively engage in the solution of the exercises. Programming is essentially a constructive and synthesizing discipline, where perfection is never going to be achieved by mere contemplation. My preference lies in simple problems—ones that are clearly formulated without an overspecification of details. The purpose and the desired form of the result should be evident without the use of intricate mathematical formalisms. Exercises should let the student become familiar with the application of the concepts and techniques discussed; they should not confront him with an ingenious puzzle whose solution requires much time and experience. The exercises at the end of each chapter serve as examples and can be varied and augmented in many ways.

The success of a programming course depends to a large extent on the organization of the available computation center. If certain minimal requirements are not met, the course can easily result in disappointment and frustration. First, a computer facility should be available that is capable of returning short jobs in a short time. Jobs occupying a processor for only a couple of seconds and producing only a few dozen lines of output should never take longer than a quarter of an hour to be returned. Secondly, the compiler system must produce intelligible replies under all circumstances. Particularly when used by novices, these replies will seldom be the expected computation results; rather, they are likely to be information about detected mistakes. The system must formulate these messages either in natural language or in the programming notation being used. Never should obscure or unmotivated operating-system messages or—even worse—octal or hexadecimal dumps appear. Commands to the local operating system must also be reduced to a minimum.

This book emerged from lecture notes used in courses at Stanford University and at the Federal Institute of Technology (ETH) in Zürich. It is therefore quite impossible to acknowledge all contributions and stimulating ideas. My special thanks go, however, to my colleagues E. W. Dijkstra (Eindhoven), C. A. R. Hoare (Belfast), and P. Naur (Copenhagen), whose contributions have not only influenced this text but the entire subject of programming. With particular gratitude, I also recall my discussions with H. Rutishauser; as the originator of the idea of programming languages and as the coauthor of ALGOL 60, he has probably had the greatest influence of all on this work. My thanks also go to Mrs. A. Forsythe for her careful reading of the manuscript. Finally, I am indebted to my collaborators

U. Ammann, E. Marmier, and R. Schild for their valiant effort in implementing a compiler for the programming language PASCAL. This effort demonstated that the notation used in this book is well suited not only to express abstract algorithms but also to produce efficient and reliable programs for real computers.

The sixth printing takes account of a revision of the programming language Pascal† that concerns the handling of textfiles. The definition of textfiles does no longer depend on the existence of explicit line control characters. This change does not necessarily imply a conceptual simplification, but represents an adaptation to widely accepted conventions.

NIKLAUS WIRTH

---

† K. Jensen and N. Wirth, PASCAL–User Manual and Report, Lecture Notes in Computer Science, Vol. 18, Springer Study Edition, Berlin, Heidelberg, New York, 1974.

SYSTEMATIC PROGRAMMING
An Introduction

1 INTRODUCTION

During the last decade, the computer has become an indispensable tool of business, industry, and scientific research in performing tasks whose treatment would be impossible without it. The computer is an automaton that executes computational processes according to precisely specified rules. It usually possesses only a limited repertoire of elementary instructions that it "understands" and is capable of obeying, but these instructions are executed with tremendous expediency and reliability. The essence of the computer's power and wide applicability lies in its ability to execute extremely long sequences of instructions containing an almost infinite combination of elementary actions. The act of incorporating such instruction sequences into "recipes" representing certain classes of computational processes is called *programming*. But the fundamental ideas behind designing programs can be explained and understood without any reference to the computer.

Programming is a discipline with many applications—one that is open to systematic methods of mathematical analysis involving plenty of non-trivial problems, and one that is above all an intellectual challenge. But the reason programming as a methodical technique has been little analyzed is because it leads to interesting applications and challenging problems, which require a solid theoretical foundation and a systematic approach, only when the programs reach a certain complexity and length (i.e., when they are composed of thousands or even millions of instructions). Before the advent of the computer, there was no "slave" willing or capable of reliably executing such long sequences of commands with absolute, thoughtless obedience; so the incentive for devising such programs was absent. Only the modern digital computer has made programming both challenging and relevant.

1

2 FUNDAMENTAL NOTIONS

This chapter will introduce some of the important basic notions of programming. Because they are fundamental, these concepts cannot formally be defined in terms of other concepts. Instead, they will be explained through the use of examples.

The most important notion is that of *action*. In this context, an action is understood to have a finite duration and to have an intended and well-defined *effect*. Each action requires the existence of some *object* on which the action is executed and on whose *changes of state* its effect can be recognized. Each action must also be describable in terms of a *language* or a system of formulas; its description is called a *statement*.

If the action can be decomposed into parts, then it is called a *process* or a *computation*. If these parts strictly follow each other in time and no two are executed simultaneously, then the process is called *sequential*. Consequently, a statement that describes a process can be broken up into parts; it is then called a *program*. A program thus consists of a set of statements whose textual ordering is not, in general, identical with the ordering in time of the corresponding actions.

The driving force that actually executes the actions according to the specified statements is called a *processor*. This rather neutral word gives no clue as to whether the agent is a human being or an automaton. Indeed, programs have meaning without reference to a specific processor so long as the underlying language is precisely defined. In general, the programmer is not interested in the identity of the processor. He need only be assured that it understands the language of his programs, for the programs are supposed to constitute the rules of behavior of the processor. The programmer therefore needs to know the kinds of statements that his available processor is capable of understanding and executing, and he must adapt his language accordingly.

2

Every action requires a certain amount of *work*, depending on the processor. This amount can be expressed as the time that it takes the processor to execute the action. This time span, in turn, can usually be more or less directly translated into a measure of cost. An experienced programmer will always take into account the capabilities of the processors available to him and will then select the solution with the least ensuing cost.

Since this text is primarily concerned with the design of programs to be executed by automatic processors (computers), the remainder of this chapter will outline some basic characteristics common to all digital computers. Preceding this bird's-eye view of computers, however, we would like to introduce two simple examples to illustrate the notions just defined.

Example: Multiplication
We are given the statement:

Multiply the two natural numbers x and y and denote their product by z.

If the available processor understands this statement, that is, if it knows what is meant by "natural number" and by "multiplication," then further elaboration is unnecessary.

For the sake of argument, however, we will assume that the available processor

(a) does not understand sentences in natural language, accepting only certain formulas, and
(b) cannot multiply but only add.

First of all, we notice that the objects of computation are natural numbers. The program, however, is not supposed to specify these numbers; rather it should specify a general *pattern of behavior* for processes multiplying arbitrary pairs of natural numbers. In place of numbers, therefore, we simply use general names denoting variable objects, called *variables*. At the beginning of each process, specific values must be assigned to these variables. This *assignment* is the most fundamental action in the computational processes executed by computers.

A variable is comparable to a blackboard: its value can be inspected ("read") as many times as desired, and it can be erased and overwritten. Overwriting, however, causes the previous value to be lost. Assignment of a value w to a variable v will subsequently be denoted by

$$v := w \tag{2.1}$$

The symbol $:=$ is called the *assignment operator*.

Formally, statement (2.1) can now be written as

$$z := x * y \tag{2.2}$$

If this statement is decomposed into a sequence of additions following each other in time, then the action of multiplication becomes a sequential process, and statement (2.3) assumes the form of a program. For the moment, this program will be formulated informally as

$$
\begin{array}{ll}
\text{Step 1:} & z := 0 \\
& u := x \\[1em]
\text{Step 2:} & \text{repeat the statements} \\
& z := z + y \\
& u := u - 1 \\
& \text{until } u = 0.
\end{array}
\tag{2.3}
$$

The process that is evoked by this program when specific values are given for x and y can be visualized by recording the values assigned to the variables u and z as the computation progresses in time. With $x = 5$ and $y = 13$, we obtain the table in (2.4).

	Values of Variables	
Step	z	u
1	0	5
2	13	4
2	26	3
2	39	2
2	52	1
2	65	0

$$\tag{2.4}$$

The process terminates, according to statement 2, as soon as $u = 0$. At this time, z has acquired the final result $65 = 5 * 13$. Such a table is called a *trace*. Note that the sequential listing of values does not mean that these values are retained; instead, each variable has at any one time exactly *one* single value. This is due to the fact that an assignment overwrites the previous value of a variable.

The objects of this computation are numbers. To perform operations on specific numbers, it is necessary to represent these numbers by a specific notation. A *choice of notation* is therefore unavoidable in executing a computation. (The program, however, is generally valid without regard to specific notation or representation of its objects.) It is also essential to distinguish between objects—even if they are abstract objects such as numbers—and their representation. In computers, for instance, numbers are usually represented by the states of magnetic storage elements, but it is highly desirable to be able to formulate processes dealing with numbers that can be obeyed by computers without reference to such magnetic states.

To illustrate these ideas and to demonstrate how the same computational process can be described by various notations, the table in (2.5) simply replaces the values in (2.4) with Roman numerals.

Step	Values of Variables	
	z	u
1	0	V
2	XIII	IV
2	XXVI	III
2	XXXIX	II
2	LII	I
2	LXV	0

(2.5)

Example : Division
We are given the instruction:

> *Divide the natural number x by the natural number y and denote the integer quotient as q and the remainder as r.*

More specifically, the following relations must hold.

$$x = q * y + r \quad \text{and} \quad 0 \leq r < y \tag{2.6.1}$$

Introducing the division operator **div**, the computation can be described by the following formal assignment statement.

$$(q, r) := x \text{ div } y \tag{2.6.2}$$

To demonstrate again the decomposition of this statement into a program, we assume that the program is to be specified for a processor incapable of division, that is, without the operator **div**. Consequently, division has to be decomposed into a sequence of subtractions of the divisor y from the dividend x, and the number of possible subtractions becomes the desired quotient q.

$$
\begin{aligned}
\text{Step 1:} \quad & q := 0 \\
& r := x \\
\text{Step 2:} \quad & \text{while } r \geq y \text{ repeat} \\
& q := q + 1 \\
& r := r - y
\end{aligned}
\tag{2.7}
$$

x and y again denote *constants* that represent given fixed values at the outset; q and r denote *variables* with integral values. The process prescribed by program (2.7), having the values $x = 100$ and $y = 15$, is listed in the trace in (2.8).

Step	Values of Variables	
	q	r
1	0	100
2	1	85
2	2	70
2	3	55
2	4	40
2	5	25
2	6	10

$$(2.8)$$

The process is terminated as soon as $r < y$. The results are $q = 6$ and $r = 10$, thus satisfying the relations (2.6.1):

$$100 = 6 * 15 + 10 \quad \text{and} \quad 0 \leq 10 < 15 \qquad (2.9)$$

These two examples are descriptions of sequential processes in which the individual assignments are performed strictly in sequential order in time. Henceforth, our discussions will be restricted to sequential processes, where the word "process" will always be understood to be an abbreviation of *sequential process*. This deliberate omission of nonsequential processes is made not only because conventional computers operate sequentially but mainly because the design of nonsequential programs—or systems of sequential but interdependent programs to be executed concurrently—is a subtle and difficult task, requiring as a basis a thorough mastery of the art of designing sequential algorithms.

These two examples also show that every program describes a sequence of state transformations of the set of its variables. If the same program is obeyed twice with different initial values (x and y), then it would be a mistake to say that the two processes or computations were the same. However, they definitely follow the same *pattern of behavior*. The description of such a pattern of behavior without reference to a particular processor is usually called an *algorithm*. The term *program* is properly used for algorithms designed so that they can be obeyed or followed by a specific processor type. The difference between a *general* (sometimes called abstract) *algorithm* and a *computer program* lies mainly in the fact that the latter must specify the rules of behavior in every little detail and must be composed according to strict notational rules. The reasons for this are the machine's limited set of instructions, which it is capable of understanding and executing, and its absolute obedience, based on its total lack of a critical attitude. These characteristics of the computer are criticized by most novices in the art of programming as the reasons behind the need for pedantic precision and attention to detail when dealing with computers. Indeed, even a trivial mistake in writing may lead to totally unintended and "meaningless" machine behavior. This obvious absence of any "common sense" to which a programmer may appeal (whenever his own senses fail) has been criticized by professionals as well, and efforts have been undertaken to remedy this seeming deficiency. The experienced programmer, however, learns to appreciate this servile attitude of the computer due to which it becomes possible to even require "unusual" patterns of behavior. For this is precisely what is impossible to ask when dealing with (human) processors who are accustomed to rounding off every instruction to the nearest interpretation that is both plausible and pleasing to them.

3 THE STRUCTURE OF COMPUTERS

To design programs executable by automatic computer, the programmer must first know his tool. The more precisely he knows his processor, the better he is able to tailor his algorithms into programs utilizing the particular capabilities of that processor. On the other hand, the more an algorithm is tailored and "tuned" to a processor, the larger the effort spent to develop the program. Under normal circumstances, a solution must be found that keeps the program-development effort within reasonable limits while still yielding sufficiently good (i.e., efficient) programs. To find such a solution, the programmer must know the kinds of adaptations that are fairly easy to perform but that, at the same time, yield a relatively large improvement. To this end, it is essential to know the most important, generally valid characteristics of computers while ignoring the idiosyncrasies and peculiarities (called features) of individual machines.

In all modern digital computers, we can distinguish between two main components.

1. The *store* (often called *memory*). The store contains the objects that are manipulated in encoded form. These encoded objects are called *data*. The performance of a store is measured by its capacity (size) and by the speed with which data can be deposited and retrieved. In any case, the store has a *finite* capacity.
2. The *processor* (arithmetic–logical unit). This unit performs additions, multiplications, comparisons, etc. Data are retrieved (read) from the store for processing, and results are deposited (written) into the store.

At each moment, the processor contains only the data to be processed immediately—that is, very few operands. Its own storage elements are called *registers*. All data that are not immediately needed are handed over to the store, which then plays the role of an "ice box."

Example : Evaluation of an expression

In order to evaluate an arithmetic expression with several operands and intermediate results, we apply again the technique of decomposing a complicated task into a sequence of simpler tasks. This causes individual arithmetic operations to take operands from the processor's registers and to replace them by the results. The evaluation of the expression

$$a * b + c * d \tag{3.1.1}$$

is broken down into simpler *instructions*:

$$\begin{aligned}
&\text{R1} := a\\
&\text{R2} := b\\
&\text{R1} := \text{R1} * \text{R2}\\
&z\ \ := \text{R1}\\
&\text{R1} := c\\
&\text{R2} := d\\
&\text{R1} := \text{R1} * \text{R2}\\
&\text{R2} := z\\
&\text{R1} := \text{R1} + \text{R2}
\end{aligned} \tag{3.1.2}$$

R1 and R2 denote the processor's registers, and z designates the intermediate result temporarily deposited in the store. The final result is made available in register R1.

The evaluation of the expression has thus been transformed into a short program consisting of three kinds of instructions or statements;

(a) instructions fetching operands from the store,
(b) (arithmetic) operations exclusively accessing processor registers, and
(c) instructions depositing results in the store.

This method of decomposing statements into more elementary steps and then temporarily saving intermediate results in the store is the reason that the same computational processes can be executed by relatively simple as well as very sophisticated computers—the former merely require more time. The decomposition method is the very essence of digital computer programming, and it is the basis for the application of relatively simple mechanisms to problems of enormous complexity. A precondition for the success of a computation consisting of billions of single steps (whose operands are always the result of previous steps) is, of course, a processor with a reasonably high speed and an absolute reliability. The realization of such processors is one of the true triumphs of modern technology.

The example of the evaluation of an expression also shows the necessity of a close interconnection between processor and store, since the amount of information flow between the two units is rather high. The store contains objects that must be accessible through distinct names (e.g., a, b, z, ...). Consequently, there must be an order in the store like that found in a set of post office boxes. The objects are therefore contained in a set of uniquely identifiable *storage cells*, each of which has a unique *address*. Each access to the store must be accompanied by a specification of the address of the cell to be referenced.

Cells in a computer store resemble storage boxes used in daily life insofar as they contain and preserve an object. But this is where the analogy ends. The ability of computer stores to preserve data is not based on the fact that they physically harbor an object, but instead that a certain *encoding* of the object is reflected by the state of the cell. The cell must therefore be capable of assuming a certain number of *discrete states*. It is difficult to realize components capable of assuming and maintaining many clearly distinguishable states over an arbitrarily long time. It is feasible, however, to build such storage elements having only two distinct states; these are called *binary* storage elements. If a group of n binary storage cells is combined, this group can assume 2^n different combinations of states. If the group is considered as an indivisible unit, then it represents a storage cell with 2^n possible states.

Example: Encoding objects into groups of binary digits

We choose the positional representation of natural numbers (including 0). A number x is encoded in the following sequence of n binary digits (called *bits*), that is, zeroes and ones,

$$x : b_{n-1} \ldots b_1 b_0 \qquad (3.2.1)$$

where the encoding rule is given by

$$x = b_0 + 2b_1 + \cdots + 2^{n-1} b_{n-1} \qquad (3.2.2)$$

This rule is by no means the only one possible, but in many respects, it is the most appropriate. After all, it is the same rule on which the representation of arabic (decimal) numbers is based; that is,

$$x : d_{m-1} \ldots d_1 d_0 \qquad (3.3.1)$$

and

$$x = d_0 + 10 * d_1 + 10^2 * d_2 + \cdots + 10^{m-1} * d_{m-1} \qquad (3.3.2)$$

Some examples of binary and decimal encodings (representations) of numbers are

Binary	Decimal	
1101	13	
10101	21	
111111	63	(3.4)
1101011	107	

The most important lesson to be learned from this example is that finite storage cells—that is, cells able to assume only a finite number of discernible states (no others exist in reality)—are capable of storing numbers only from a *finite range of values*. In a computer the number of binary storage elements grouped into a single addressable storage cell (word) is usually called the *wordlength*. The capabilities of the arithmetic unit are adapted to this measure. Common values of wordlengths n are 8, 16, 24, 32, 48 and 64 with corresponding sets of 2^n distinct values.

The consequence of the basic requirement that the computer must be able to obey a given program is that it must have "easy" access to that program. Where, then, is the most appropriate place to hold a program? It was the brilliant—and nowadays seemingly trivial—idea of *John von Neumann* to put the program into the store. Consequently, the same store is used to hold both the objects and the "recipe" of the computing processes, that is, the data *and* the program.

Obviously, this concept of the *stored-program computer* requires that instructions also be encoded. In our example of an expression evaluation every instruction is representable by an *operation code* (to specify reading, writing, adding, multiplying, etc.) and, in some cases, by an operand. If operands are represented by storage-cell addresses and if these addresses are chosen to be the whole numbers $0, 1, 2, \ldots$, then the problem of encoding programs is essentially solved; every program can be represented by sequences of numbers (or groups of numbers) and can therefore be deposited in a computer's store.

Another consequence of the stored-program approach is that every program will occupy a certain number of storage cells, that is, a certain amount of *storage space*. The number of occupied cells, which are no longer available to hold data, is proportional to the length of the program text. The programmer must therefore aim to keep his programs as concise as possible.

The following, important capabilities of the modern digital computer are based on the concept of sharing the store between the program and the data.

1. As soon as execution of a certain program P is terminated, a new program Q can be accepted in the store for subsequent execution (flexibility, wide applicability).
2. A computer may generate (according to a certain program) a sequence of numbers that it will subsequently consider and interpret as encoded instructions. Data generated in the first step become the program obeyed in the second step.
3. A computer X may be instructed to consider sequences of numbers actually representing programs as data to be transformed (according to some translation program) into sequences of numbers representing programs encoded for a different computer Y.

4 PROGRAMMING AIDS AND SYSTEMS

Until the late 1950s, programming consisted of the detailed encoding of long sequences of instructions—initially written in some symbolic notation—into numbers in binary, octal, or hexadecimal form. This activity is called *coding* in contrast to programming, which encompasses the more difficult task of designing algorithms. The inadequacies of this cumbersome procedure became more and more apparent with the advent of faster computers having larger stores.

1. The coder was forced to tailor his programs to the particular characteristics of his available computer. He therefore had to consider all details of the machine, including its processor organization and its instruction set. The exchange of programs between various machines was impossible, and even the most thorough knowledge of coding methods on one machine was fairly useless when applied to another computer. Every institute designed programs of its own and was forced to dispose of them and to code new ones whenever a new computer replaced the old one. It became evident that the adaptation and tuning of algorithms to the peculiar characteristics of a specific computer represented an unwise investment of human intellect.

2. The close binding of the programmer to one type of computer not only enabled but even encouraged the invention and application of all kinds of tricks to gain maximum machine performance. While this "trickology" was still considered the essence of good programming, the programmer spent considerable time in the construction of "optimal" codes, whose verification was generally very difficult. It was practically impossible to discover the principles of a program designed by a colleague—and often as difficult to explain those of one's own programs! This artistry of coding has now lost most of its glory. The experienced programmer

12

consciously avoids the use of tricks, choosing systematic and transparent solutions instead.

3. The so-called *machine code* contained only a minimal amount of redundancy on the basis of which formal coding errors could be detected. As a result, even typing errors, which could have devastating effects when the program was executed, were difficult and time consuming to discover.

4. The representation of a complex program as an unstructured, linear sequence of commands was a most inappropriate form for the human inspector to comprehend and to express. We will show later that the presence and application of structure is the principal tool in helping the programmer to synthesize systematically and to maintain an overall comprehension of complicated programs.

These shortcomings led to the development of the so-called "high level" *programming languages.* Such languages became the means through which to instruct an idealized, hypothetical computer that is designed not according to the limitations of current technology but according to the habits and the capabilities of man to express his thoughts. In this situation, however, we are confronted with a machine A, which is economically realizable but neither convenient nor encouraging to use, and a computer B, which is suited to human needs but exists only on paper. The gap between these two kinds of objects is now bridged by an entity called *software.* (In contrast, the physical machine is called *hardware.*) A software system is a *program C* that, when executed by the existing computer A, enables A to translate programs written for the hypothetical machine B into programs of its own. Program C is called a translator or *compiler*; it enables A to appear as the idealized machine B.

The utilization of compiler C thus relieves the programmer of the burden of considering the particular, detailed characteristics of his computer A. But it does not free him of the duty to be constantly aware that it is machine A that will ultimately execute his programs and that A has some *definite limitations*, imposed by its finite speed and storage capacity.

Usually, a combined hardware–software system processes programs P in two distinct steps, which follow each other in time. During the first step, P is translated by the compiler C into a form interpretable by A; this step is called *compilation.* In the second step, the translated program is executed; this step is called *execution.*

Compilation: program = compiler C
input data = program P in language B
output data = program P in language A

Execution: program = P in language A
input data = arguments of computation X
output data = computational results Y

5 SOME SIMPLE PROGRAMS

Chapter 4 showed clearly why a program must consist of statements formulated in a notation that the computer "understands." Although we do not know yet which kinds of statements and formulas a programming language contains, we do know that these statements will precisely specify the intended actions. This unquestionable necessity for precision probably constitutes the main difference between communication among humans and communication with machines. Work with computers requires both precision and clarity. Vagueness and ambiguity are strictly forbidden.

A commonly used and easily comprehended notation to express programs is the so-called *flow-diagram* or flowchart. Program (2.3) is depicted in (5.1) as a flow-diagram.

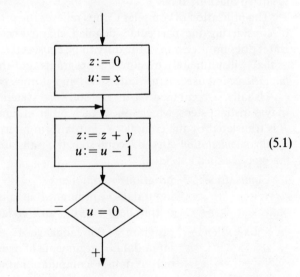

$$\begin{aligned} z &:= 0 \\ u &:= x \end{aligned}$$

$$\begin{aligned} z &:= z + y \\ u &:= u - 1 \end{aligned}$$

$$u = 0$$

(5.1)

This pictorial representation clearly displays the possible sequence of steps by visually illustrating two kinds of instructions:

(a) the assignment of values to variables, denoted by rectangles, and
(b) the decisions, denoted by diamonds.

A decision step has more than one possible successor. If the specified relation or condition is satisfied, then the path denoted by the $+$ sign is followed; otherwise the one denoted by the $-$ sign is taken. A repetition manifests itself by a *loop*, that is, a closed sequence consisting of statements and at least one decision that will determine the termination of the repetition. In the same fashion, program (2.7) is represented by flow-diagram (5.2).

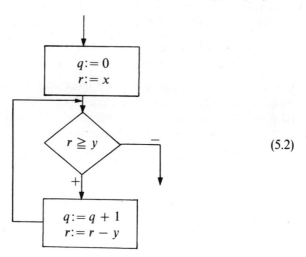

(5.2)

A program determines a pattern of behavior for an unspecified, often infinite number of possible processes. The individual processes are distinguished by the values of the variables involved at related time intervals and, in particular, by the *initial values* or arguments. But how can we ensure that all processes executable according to a given program will compute the specified results? This question of the *correctness of programs* is one of the most central, crucial, and unavoidable issues of programming.

The correctness of programs (2.3) and (2.7) was demonstrated in tables (2.4) and (2.8) for a fixed pair of values x and y. This method of establishing correctness is called *program testing*; it consists of selecting arguments (x and y), executing the process with these selected arguments, and comparing the computed results with the previously known correct results. This experimental testing is repeated with several arguments, using the computer as the ideal tool. Nevertheless, this conventional method is expensive, time consuming, and cumbersome. In the end, it is also unsatisfactory, since to remove all doubts about the correctness of a program, it would be necessary to execute all possible computations—not just a selected few. But if the results of all processes have to be known beforehand, there would hardly be any purpose in writing a computer program. Anyway, in practice, such an exhaustive testing of a program is quite impossible. For example: Assume that a given computer takes 1 μsec for the addition of two numbers (according to its program) and that it is capable of representing numbers up to an absolute value of 2^{60}. Then 2^{2*60} different additions are possible, taking

$$2^{2*60} * 10^{-6} \sec \doteq 3.2 * 10^{22} \text{ yr}$$

Since this kind of exhaustive experimental testing is both senseless and impossible, we can formulate an important ground rule.

> *Experimental testing of programs can be used to show the presence of errors but never to prove their absence.*

Consequently, it is necessary to abstract from individual processes and to postulate certain generally valid conditions that can be derived from the pattern of behavior. This analytic method of testing is called *program verification*. In contrast to program testing—where the properties of individual *processes* are investigated—program verification is concerned with the properties of the *program*.

Program verification employs the same principles as empirical testing and might therefore be considered analogous with process verification. But instead of recording the individual values of variables in a trace table, we postulate generally valid ranges of values and relationships among variables after each statement. "Generally valid" should be understood to mean "valid for each process executable according to the given program and valid at the point of annotation irrespective of the statements previously obeyed." We can now postulate four basic *rules of analytic program verification*.

1. Preceding and succeeding every statement, one or several conditions are specified that are satisfied before and after every execution of the statement. The annotated conditions are called *assertions*; the ones preceding a statement S are called its *antecedents* P; and the ones following it are called consequences or *consequents* Q.

$$
\begin{array}{l}
\mid --- P \text{ (antecedent)} \\
\downarrow \\
\boxed{\quad S \quad} \\
\mid --- Q \text{ (consequent)} \\
\downarrow
\end{array}
\qquad (5.3)
$$

2. If several paths of a flow-diagram merge in front of a statement T, then the consequents Q_i of all preceding statements S_i must logically imply the antecedent P of statement T. Thus

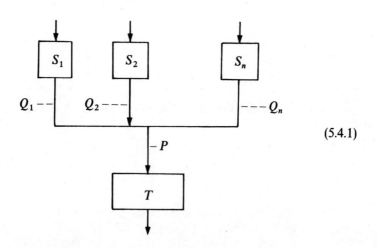

(5.4.1)

$$Q_i \supset P \quad \text{for} \quad i = 1 \ldots n$$
$(Q \supset P$ is verbalized as "Q implies P.")

Example:

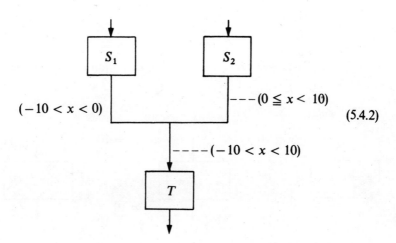

(5.4.2)

3. If an assertion P holds preceding a decision with condition B, then the two consequents are

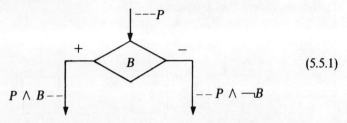

$$P \wedge B \qquad\qquad\qquad P \wedge \neg B \qquad\qquad (5.5.1)$$

($P \wedge B$ is verbalized as "P and B," $P \wedge \neg B$ as "P and not B.")

Example:

$$-10 < x < 10$$

$$x < 0 \qquad\qquad\qquad (5.5.2)$$

$$-10 < x < 0 \qquad\qquad\qquad -0 \leqq x < 10$$

4. If an assertion P holds after the assignment of the value w to the variable v, the antecedent of the assignment is obtained by substituting w for all free occurrences of v in P.

$$--- P_w^v$$

$$\boxed{v := w} \qquad\qquad (5.6.1)$$

$$--- P$$

(This rule may well be regarded as the definition of the *effect of assignment*.)

Examples:

$$-- x + y = 10 \qquad\quad --- x + 1 = 10 \qquad\quad -- f(x) = u$$

$$\boxed{z := x + y} \qquad\quad \boxed{x := x + 1} \qquad\quad \boxed{x := f(x)}$$

$$-- z = 10 \qquad\qquad ---- x = 10 \qquad\qquad - x = u$$

$$(5.6.2)$$

$$\vert ----- y = x^2, \quad d = 2x - 1, \quad d + 2 = 2x + 1$$

$\boxed{d := d + 2}$

$$\vert ------ y = x^2, \quad d = 2x + 1, \quad y + d = (x + 1)^2$$

$\boxed{y := y + d}$

$$\vert -------- y = (x + 1)^2, \quad d = 2x + 1, \quad d + 2 = 2(x + 1) + 1$$

$\boxed{d := d + 2}$

$$\vert ------ y = (x + 1)^2, \quad d = 2(x + 1) + 1, \quad y + d = (x + 2)^2$$

$\boxed{y := y + d}$

$$\vert ------ y = (x + 2)^2, \quad d = 2(x + 2) - 1$$

$$(5.7)$$

We will now apply these basic rules in verifying the correctness of programs (5.1) and (5.2), which compute the product and quotient of two natural numbers, respectively. First, we establish the following intermediate results by applying the derivation rule for the assignment statement.

$$\vert ----- \begin{cases} z + u * y = z + y + (u - 1) * y = x * y \\ u > 0 \end{cases}$$

$\boxed{z := z + y}$

$$\vert ---- z + (u - 1) * y = x * y, \quad u - 1 \geq 0 \qquad (5.8)$$

$\boxed{u := u - 1}$

$$\vert ----- z + u * y = x * y, \quad u \geq 0$$

$$\vert ----- \begin{cases} r + q * y = r - y + (q + 1) * y = x \\ r - y \geq 0 \end{cases}$$

$\boxed{r := r - y}$

$$\vert ---- r + (q + 1) * y = x, r \geq 0 \qquad (5.9)$$

$\boxed{q := q + 1}$

$$\vert ----- r + q * y = x, \quad r \geq 0$$

The two complete programs with the relevant assertions are shown in flow-diagrams (5.10) and (5.11).

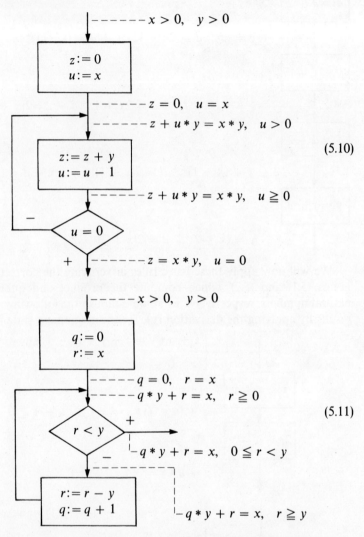

$$-----x > 0, \quad y > 0$$

(inside box) $z := 0$
$u := x$

$$------z = 0, \quad u = x$$
$$------z + u*y = x*y, \quad u > 0$$

(5.10)

(inside box) $z := z + y$
$u := u - 1$

$$------z + u*y = x*y, \quad u \geq 0$$

(diamond) $u = 0$

$$------z = x*y, \quad u = 0$$

$$-----x > 0, \quad y > 0$$

(inside box) $q := 0$
$r := x$

$$-----q = 0, \quad r = x$$
$$-----q*y + r = x, \quad r \geq 0$$

(5.11)

(diamond) $r < y$

$$-q*y + r = x, \quad 0 \leq r < y$$

(inside box) $r := r - y$
$q := q + 1$

$$-q*y + r = x, \quad r \geq y$$

The determination of assertions in a sequence of statements, based on rules (5.3)–(5.7), is generally a straightforward matter, when either the antecedent of the first statement or the consequent of the last statement is given. A serious difficulty arises, however, as soon as the flow-diagram contains closed circular paths, that is, if the program contains repetitions. In this case, the best approach is to cut the loop at some place and then postulate a *hypothesis H* at the cut. Starting with the hypothesis, assertions can be derived through the now linearized sequence, going either forward or backward. The resulting assertion P_n at the end (i.e., at the cut) must then logically imply (or be implied by) H so that the cut may be closed. If this is not satisfied, another hypothesis must be assumed, and the process must be repeated, as shown in (5.12).

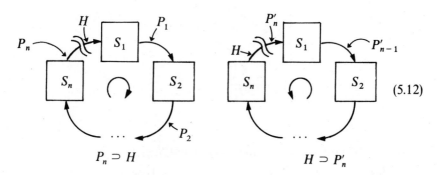

$$P_n \supset H \qquad\qquad\qquad H \supset P'_n$$

(5.12)

It is advantageous to place the cut preceding the condition B according to which the repetition is terminated. The logical combination of conditions H and B will then constitute the consequent of the entire repetitive statement group.

Such an assertion, holding independently of the number of previously executed repetitions, is called a loop-invariant or simply an *invariant*, since it represents a condition that does not change while the process progresses. In programs (5.10) and (5.11), the two invariants are, respectively,

$$(z + u * y = x * y) \wedge (u \geq 0)$$

and

$$(q * y + r = x) \wedge (r \geq 0)$$

Since repetitions or loops are fundamental constituents in all computational processes and computer programs, we can formulate these instructions as *rules of derivation*. These rules specify the consequent of a repetitive statement, given its antecedent and given the assertions for the statement that is repeated.

1. Given an assertion P that is invariant over statement S—that is, if given as its antecedent, it is also its consequent—and is represented by

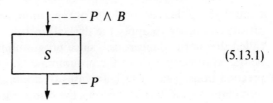

(5.13.1)

we can make the following assertion about the repetitive statement S' :

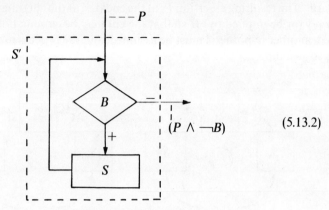

$$(5.13.2)$$

2. Given the two preconditions about statement S,

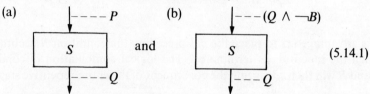

$$(5.14.1)$$

we can make the following assertion about the repetitive statement S'' :

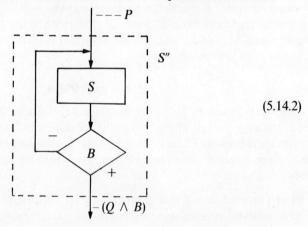

$$(5.14.2)$$

Note that for this second form of repetition, *two* preconditions must be satisfied in order to apply the derivation rule. This form may justly be called the more "dangerous," since programming errors may frequently be traced directly back to the programmer's oversight of one of the two preconditions [usually (a)]. In cases of doubt, the first form, where the termination condition B precedes the statement S, is recommended.

These guidelines should be considered essentially as an informal approach to the problem of analytic verification of the properties of programs. It is particularly important to realize the difficulties involved in the problem of finding invariants. The lesson that every programmer should learn is that the *explicit indication of the relevant invariant for each repetition represents the most valuable element in every program documentation.* But even if a program is intended for the exclusive use of its author, the explicit determination of invariants may help in preventing many errors, which otherwise would be discovered only by extensive testing, and often even remain a permanent "feature" of the supposedly correct program. Just as important, however, is the explicit indication of the variables' ranges of values, particularly those for the initial values for which the stated program properties hold.

Finally, figures (5.15) and (5.16) demonstrate what constitutes both a necessary and an adequate program documentation. It is important to remember that a program may be *overdocumented.* A program containing so many comments that the actual statements are difficult to spot is useless!

Multiplication of natural numbers

Arguments: x, y
Result: z
Auxiliary variable: u

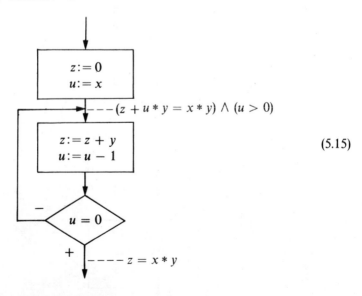

$$z := 0$$
$$u := x$$

$$- - - (z + u * y = x * y) \wedge (u > 0)$$

$$z := z + y$$
$$u := u - 1$$

(5.15)

$$u = 0$$

$$- - - - z = x * y$$

Division of natural numbers

Arguments: x, y
Results: q (integer quotient), r (remainder)

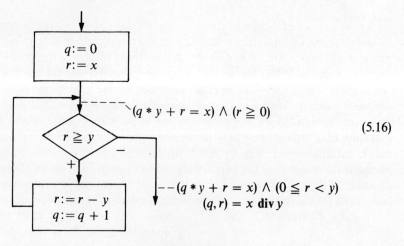

$$(q*y + r = x) \wedge (r \geqq 0)$$

$$(q*y + r = x) \wedge (0 \leqq r < y)$$
$$(q, r) = x \text{ div } y$$

(5.16)

EXERCISES

5.1 The following program computes the product $z := x * y$, where only the operations of addition, doubling, and halving are employed. The arguments x and y are natural numbers; u and v are (auxiliary) integer variables. The predicate $odd(u)$

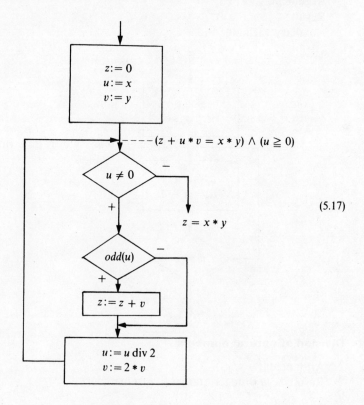

$$(z + u*v = x*y) \wedge (u \geqq 0)$$

$$z = x * y$$

(5.17)

is satisfied if u is an odd number. Determine the relevant antecedents and consequents of each statement that can be derived by applying rules (5.3)–(5.6) from the given invariant.

5.2 The following program computes the greatest common divisor (GCD) of two natural numbers x and y; a and b are integer variables whose final value represents the desired result.

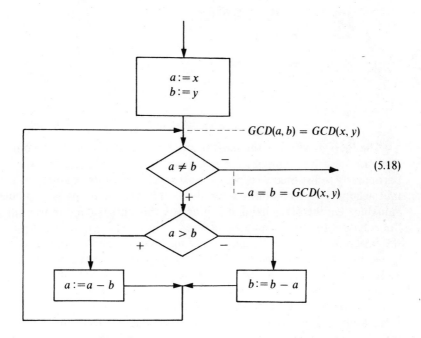

As in Exercise 5.1, determine the necessary assertions by using these known relationships of the function GCD:

(a) $u > v: GCD(u, v) = GCD(u - v, v)$
(b) $GCD(u, v) = GCD(v, u)$
(c) $GCD(u, u) = u$

5.3 Following the pattern in program (5.17), design a program to compute $z = x^y$ for the given natural numbers x and y. Include the necessary assertions to verify the correctness of your program.

6 FINITENESS OF PROGRAMS

The loop structure is the most characteristic element in every computer program because it implies the *repetition* of an action, and automata are particularly well suited to repetitive tasks. The computer's ability to maintain accuracy and reliability after thousands of repetitions is particularly valuable. On the other hand, it is precisely this untiring and indiscriminate "obedience" to a program that requires an increased caution on the part of the programmer. Consequently, one important property required of every program is that it *terminates* after a *finite* number of repetitions. Unfortunately, processes that do not terminate are a fairly common and costly phenomenon in computer installations everywhere. These can be avoided, however, through an increased meticulousness during program design and verification. To explain the precautions necessary to ensure termination, we can use the fundamental loop structure shown in (6.1).

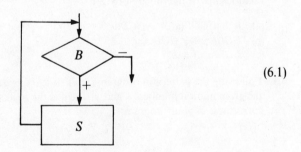

$$(6.1)$$

A minimal requirement for termination is that statement S must change the value of one or more variables in such a way that after a finite number of passes, condition B can no longer be satisfied. In general, the finiteness of a repetition can be formally derived by postulating an integer function N, depending on certain variables of the program, and by showing that

(a) if B is satisfied, then $N > 0$ and
(b) each execution of S decreases the value of N.

The application of this rule is trivial in the case of program (5.2). Statement S is

$$r := r - y$$
$$q := q + 1$$

and condition B is

$$r \geq y$$

where r, q, and y are natural numbers. We choose $N = r - y$. Since

(a) $r \geq y$ implies $N \geq 0$ and
(b) the execution of S decreases the value of r and therefore of N, finiteness is evidently guaranteed. Note, in particular, the necessity of the initial condition $y > 0$.

As a second example, we can use the application of the derivation rule to program (5.18). Its statement S consists of two alternatives,

$$a := a - b \quad \text{if } a > b, \quad \text{or} \quad b := b - a \quad \text{if } b > a$$

and condition B is $a = b$. Again, a and b are natural numbers with initial values $a > 0$, $b > 0$, and $a \neq b$. A suitable choice for $N(a, b)$ turns out to be $N = \max(a, b)$. The effect of S upon N must be considered in two separate cases. If $a > b$, then b remains unchanged and a is decreased by b. Since $a > 0$, $b > 0$, and $a \neq b$ initially, the first two relations remain unchanged (invariant) and N decreases. If $b > a$, then a remains unchanged and $b = \max(a, b) = N$ decreased by a. Thus since $N = \max(a, b)$ decreases during each repetition and, on the other hand, $\min(a, b)$ remains positive, it follows that at some time, $\max(a, b) = \min(a, b)$, and therefore $a \neq b$ is no longer satisfied. This terminates the repetition.

EXERCISES

6.1 Determine the range of values of x and y that will guarantee the finiteness of the programs in Exercises 5.1 and 5.3.

6.2 For which range of values of x and y is the following program finite?

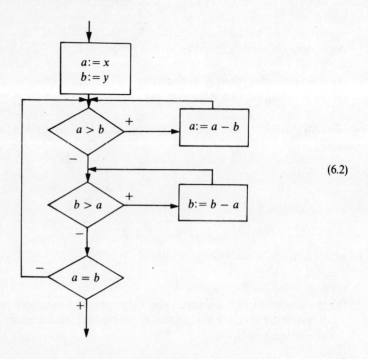

(6.2)

6.3 In which cases does program (6.2) compute the greatest common divisor of x and y? Determine the necessary and sufficient assertions.

7 SEQUENTIAL NOTATION AND PROGRAMMING LANGUAGES

7.1 SURVEY

When programs are ready to be processed by a computer, they must not be in the form of flow-diagrams. These two-dimensional, pictorial representations cannot be accepted by conventional input devices. Programs in the form of flow-diagrams must therefore be translated into machine-readable form before they can be executed. Since such translation is a likely source of errors, it is highly desirable to represent the program in a form that is not only machine-readable but also well defined and convenient for the programmer to work with. In so doing, this representation serves as the *original form* in which a program is conceived, thereby avoiding the crucial question of which representation (diagram or translation) constitutes the valid definition of the algorithm.

The most widespread data input devices are punched card readers and typewriters (which sometimes use punched paper tape). In both cases, the given data take the form of a *linear sequence of printable characters*, that is, the form of a sequential or serial text. Textual notations for programs are usually called *programming languages*. They are designed according to certain rules, which precisely define the set of correct sentences or statements. The set of such rules is called a *syntax*. Since programs formulated in these languages are to be read and understood by automata with a relatively narrow range of understanding, a strict enforcement of these syntax rules is not surprising. To learn a programming language therefore requires both a comprehension of the meaning of the available forms of sentences and a detailed knowledge of the syntactic rules governing the language. The latter usually assumes a larger proportion of attention than is customary in learning natural languages, since programs must not only be read and understood but, more importantly, be invented and formulated.

Disregarding trivial programming problems, the main effort in constructing a program lies in the conception and verification of the underlying algorithm—the effort required to formulate it in a specific notation is comparatively small. The development of an algorithm is often a complex and time-consuming process during which the final solution is approximated in steps. At each step, the program is specified in more detail. Obviously, the notation used should be suited to the problem as much as possible, but it need not assume the machine-readable appearance of a formal language. It may very well take the form of a flow-diagram, a mathematical formula, or even a natural language. However, the final step must produce a program that has been formulated in a programming language, a goal that necessarily influences the direction of the whole step-by-step development process. Consequently, it is essential that such notation be introduced at the outset of a programming course.

The coding of an algorithm in a certain machine code is a complex task, but it can be well mechanized. Tools to automate machine coding are therefore highly desirable. Particularly useful is a language that contains all the fundamental and most frequently encountered concepts of programming, allowing the expression of these concepts in a clear and natural manner, and that also permits an economical and efficient computer processing. Efforts to design such languages—both programmer and machine oriented—were often influenced by a specific area of application, an available type of computer, or both. The subject of numerical mathematics was predestined for the design of such a language, since it allowed to a large extent the adoption of traditional and proven formal notations of mathematics. These ideas were first pursued and formulated in 1952 by *H. Rutishauser*, but they found widespread acceptance and use only after 1957, when IBM published a programming language called FORTRAN and released a compiler (FORmula TRANslator) that translated programs automatically into machine code. This made the use of such a language both theoretically interesting and practically feasible. However, the form of FORTRAN was obviously oriented to a certain type of computer manufactured by IBM. The language was therefore organized and defined in a manner that left room for improvement.†

In 1958 the original ideas of H. Rutishauser were taken up by an international group of experts and condensed into the definition of a programming language. It was called ALGOL (for ALGOrithmic Language) and became the predecessor of the language ALGOL 60, which was subsequently widely used in scientific applications. ALGOL 60 was defined in 1960 by an international group of 13 scientists and edited into a report by *P. Naur*.[1] One of

---

† U.S.A. Standard FORTRAN, USA Standards Inst., New York, 1966.

[1] P. Naur, "Revised Report on the Algorithmic Language ALGOL 60," *Comm. ACM* 6 (1963), 1–17; *Comp. J.* 5 (1962–1963), 349–367; *Numer. Math.* 4 (1963), 420–453.

R. Baumann, M. Feliciano, F. L. Bauer, and K. Samelson, "Introduction to ALGOL", Prentice-Hall, Inc., 1964.

the characteristics that favorably distinguishes ALGOL from FORTRAN is that the former is precisely and concisely defined by a relatively short document; and instead of being oriented towards a specific computer, ALGOL adopts largely mathematical notation already familiar to scientists and engineers. To define the syntactical rules, a formalism was introduced that allows one to determine algorithmically whether a certain construct is a legal sentence of the language. This notation, known as *Backus-Naur-Formalism* (BNF), was later used in the definition of other programming languages.

Similar efforts to postulate a common problem-oriented language were undertaken in the area of commercial data processing. Under the auspices of the U.S. Department of Defense, the programming language COBOL (COmmon Business Oriented Language) was developed in 1962.†† It was tailored to the needs, problem areas, and habits of expression of programmers in commercial data processing. Today, COBOL is one—if not the—most frequently used language, but ranks even lower than FORTRAN in such aspects as precise definition, systematic structure, and general applicability.

A negative result of the rapid spread of these early languages was the division of programming into scientific and commercial applications. Because programming was considered to consist mainly of coding algorithms in a specific language, the notion that so-called scientific and commercial programmers should be trained separately became all too common. In fact, however, the fundamental ideas of program design and the elementary objects to be processed are quite independent of any area of application.

An effort to "reunite" the two camps by a common language was made by IBM between 1964–1967: a language was defined and subsequently supported that was supposed to be not only independent of any particular computer but also uniformly applicable to any problem area. It became known as PL/I. The language itself as well as its description have assumed remarkable dimensions, and PL/I seems to be ill suited as a basic introduction to programming because of its sheer size (precluding the possibility of complete mastery) and its lack of a systematic structure with a unifying underlying conception.

Following the notion that a programming course should primarily teach the design of algorithms and only secondarily be concerned with aspects of coding, we choose here a notation that is not identical to any of the previously mentioned languages. It was designed specifically to mirror the most fundamental concepts of programs in a natural, perspicuous, and concise form. Moreover, its syntactic rules are simple, systematic, and suitable for automatic processing. The notation is designed and defined as a close approximation to ALGOL 60, so it could appropriately be called an extension of ALGOL 60.[2] We will introduce specific elements of the language—in logical order—

---

†† U.S.A. Standard COBOL, USA Standards Inst., New York, 1968.
[2] N. Wirth, "The Programming Language PASCAL," *Acta Informatica*, 1 (1971), 35–63.

whenever the corresponding concepts become relevant to the subject being discussed. Consequently, only the general rules defining the syntactic structure of languages will be discussed here.

Every language is based on a *vocabulary*. Sentences—in this case, programs—are composed by concatenating *basic symbols* from this vocabulary according to the *syntactic rules* of the language definition. The vocabulary[3] usually consists of letters, digits, and special symbols (e.g., $+, -, *$). Because the set of special symbols is usually quite large in programming languages, natural English words are often used to denote them to increase readability. To make it clear, however, that these words (called *word-delimiters*) are not an ordinary sequence of letters but a basic symbol, they usually appear in boldface type (e.g., **begin, end**).

The syntax (see Appendix A) is formulated in a manner that allows one to verify easily whether a given sequence of symbols is a correct sentence of the language. The rules take the form of flow-diagrams and are called *syntax-diagrams*. The possible paths represent the possible symbol sequences. Starting with the diagram labeled "program," a path is traversed either by transferring to another diagram, if a rectangle is encountered, or by reading the basic symbol S, if a circle enclosing S is encountered. For example:

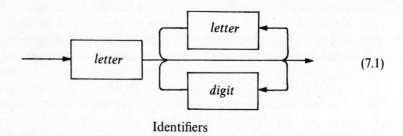

(7.1)

Identifiers

From diagram (7.1), the following sequences of letters and digits (among many others) emerge as possible identifiers.

a
abcdef
a15
q2p9
Appollo

Conversely, the following clearly cannot be classified as identifiers,

word-delimiter
J. F. Kennedy
7x

---

[3] The complete vocabulary for the PASCAL notation is listed in Appendix A.

7.2 EXPRESSIONS AND STATEMENTS

The syntax of a language defines certain sentential constructs. Among the most important are the expression and the statement, which are present in practically all programming languages.

An *expression* is a formula or rule of computation that always specifies a *value* or result. An expression consists of *operands* and *operators*. The operands are either constants (e.g., numbers), variables, or values generated by functions. Operators are usually classified as *monadic* or *dyadic*, having one or two operands, respectively. If several operators occur in an expression, the sequence of their execution must be specified. This can be done either by explicit parentheses or by implicit rules of the language. In most languages, the dyadic operators are further subdivided into (at least) two classes: additive and multiplicative operators. The latter are given a higher priority or binding strength. Furthermore, we will assume that sequences of operators of equal priority will always be executed in order from left to right. These simple rules are illustrated by the following examples.

$$
\begin{aligned}
x + y + z \quad & = (x + y) + z \\
x * y + z \quad & = (x * y) + z \\
x + y * z \quad & = x + (y * z) \\
x - y * z - w & = (x - (y * z)) - w \qquad (7.2) \\
x * y - z * w & = (x * y) - (z * w) \\
-x + y/z \quad & = (-x) + (y/z) \\
x * y/z \quad\;\; & = (x * y)/z \\
x/y * z \quad\;\; & = (x/y) * z
\end{aligned}
$$

The most elementary form of *statement* is the assignment statement. It is represented by

$$
V := E \qquad (7.3)
$$

where V denotes a variable and E an expression. Whereas an expression has a value, a statement has an *effect*.

Sequences of statements (compound statements), conditional, and repetitive statements are expressed by constructs called *structured statements*. We will introduce six basic forms of frequently occurring composite statements. Their meaning is described by the equivalent flow-diagrams.

Compound statements

$$\textbf{begin } S1; S2; \ldots; Sn \textbf{ end} \tag{7.4}$$

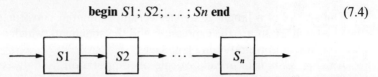

The separator "$;$" is a sequencing operator; it causes the subsequent state-ment to be executed only after the preceding one is terminated. The basic symbols **begin** and **end** represent "fat" parentheses or the so-called *statement parentheses*. Since sequences of statements often assume a considerable textual length, it is appropriate to use highly visible parentheses to emphasize the grouping of the component statements.

Conditional statements

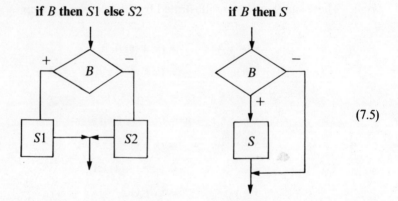

The second form may be considered to be an abbreviation of the first in which the alternative $S2$ is empty.

The role of the statement parentheses is illustrated by the following example:

$$\textbf{if } B \textbf{ then } S1; S2 \tag{7.6.1}$$

denotes the same program as

$$\textbf{begin if } B \textbf{ then } S1 \textbf{ end}; S2 \tag{7.6.2}$$

but not the same as

$$\textbf{if } B \textbf{ then begin } S1; S2 \textbf{ end} \tag{7.6.3}$$

Repetitive statements

while B **do** S **repeat** S **until** B

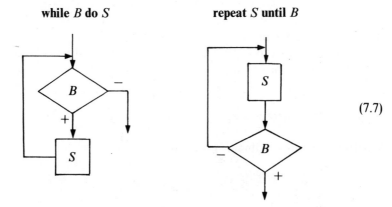

(7.7)

Note: Since the two basic symbols **repeat** and **until** already constitute a pair of brackets, the form
$$\textbf{repeat } S1\,;\, S2\,;\dots\,;\, Sn \textbf{ until } B$$
is admissible without an additional **begin–end** pair.

Selective statements
$$\textbf{case } i \textbf{ of } L1:S1\,;\, L2:S2\,;\dots\,;\, Ln:Sn \textbf{ end}$$

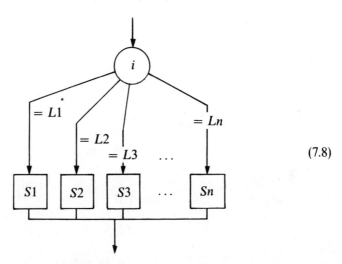

(7.8)

In case the expression i has the value L_k, the statement S_k is selected and executed; $L_i \neq L_j$ for $i \neq j$. *Note*: If $S_i = S_j = \cdots = S_k$, we use the notation $L_i, L_j, \dots L_k : S$ as an abbreviation.

As in flow-diagram notation, annotation of a program by comments and assertions should be easy. For this purpose, we introduce the convention that any text enclosed by curly braces { and } should be considered a non-executable commentary and may therefore be ignored by a processor. Now it becomes possible to express the elementary verification derivation rules in terms of program schemas in linear notation.[4] The common form is

$$\{P\} \quad S \quad \{Q\}$$

where P is the antecedent and Q the consequent of statement S.

Verification rules in linear notation

1. Assignment statement

$$\{P_w^v\} \; v := w \; \{P\} \tag{7.9}$$

   (See 5.6.1.)

2. Compound statement

   Preconditions: $\quad \{P\} \; S1 \; \{Q\}$ (7.10)

   $\{Q\} \; S2 \; \{R\}$

   Consequence: $\quad \{P\} \; S1 ; S2 \; \{R\}$

3. Conditional statements

   Preconditions: $\quad \{P \wedge B\} \; S1 \; \{Q\}$ (7.11)

   $\{P \wedge \neg B\} \; S2 \; \{Q\}$

   Consequence: $\quad \{P\}$ **if** B **then** $S1$ **else** $S2 \; \{Q\}$

   Preconditions: $\quad \{P \wedge B\} \; S \; \{Q\}$ (7.12)

   $(P \wedge \neg B) \supset Q$

   Consequence: $\quad \{P\}$ **if** B **then** $S \; \{Q\}$

4. Repetitive statements

   Precondition: $\quad \{P \wedge B\} \; S \; \{P\}$ (7.13)

   Consequence: $\quad \{P\}$ **while** B **do** $S \; \{P \wedge \neg B\}$

   Preconditions: $\quad \{P\} \; S \; \{Q\}$

   $\{Q \wedge \neg B\} \; S \; \{Q\}$ (7.14)

   Consequence: $\quad \{P\}$ **repeat** S **until** $B \; \{Q \wedge B\}$

5. Selective statement

   Preconditions: $\quad \{P \wedge (i = L_k)\} \; S_k \; \{Q\}$ for all k

   Consequence: $\quad \{P\}$ **case** i **of**

   $L1 : S1 ;$

   $L2 : S2 ;$ (7.15)

   . . .

   $Ln : Sn$ **end** $\{Q\}$

(The consequence holds only if $i = L_k$ for some k.)

---

[4] C. A. R. Hoare, "An Axiomatic Basis for Computer Programming," *Comm. ACM* 12 (Oct. 1969), 576–583.

7.3 SIMPLE PROGRAMS IN SEQUENTIAL NOTATION

The notational devices introduced so far can now be used to express programs discussed in previous chapters in terms of sequential programming language.

Multiplication of two natural numbers
(cf. 5.15)

$$\begin{aligned}
&\textbf{begin } z := 0; u := x; \\
&\quad \textbf{repeat } \{z + u * y = x * y, u > 0\} \\
&\qquad z := z + y; u := u - 1 \\
&\quad \textbf{until } u = 0 \\
&\textbf{end}
\end{aligned}$$
(7.16)

Integer division of two natural numbers
(cf. 5.16)

$$\begin{aligned}
&\textbf{begin } q := 0; r := x; \\
&\quad \textbf{while } r \geqq y \textbf{ do} \\
&\quad \textbf{begin } \{q * y + r = x, r \geqq y\} \\
&\qquad r := r - y; q := q + 1 \\
&\quad \textbf{end} \\
&\textbf{end}
\end{aligned}$$
(7.17)

Multiplication of two natural numbers
(cf. 5.17)

$$\begin{aligned}
&\textbf{begin } z := 0; u := x; v := y; \\
&\quad \textbf{while } u \neq 0 \textbf{ do} \\
&\quad \textbf{begin } \{z + u * v = x * y, u > 0\} \\
&\qquad \textbf{if } odd(u) \textbf{ then } z := z + v; \\
&\qquad u := u \textbf{ div } 2; v := 2 * v \\
&\quad \textbf{end} \\
&\quad \{z = x * y\} \\
&\textbf{end}
\end{aligned}$$
(7.18)

Computation of the greatest common divisor
(cf. 5.18)

$$\begin{aligned}
&\textbf{begin } a := x; b := y; \\
&\quad \textbf{while } a \neq b \textbf{ do} \\
&\quad \textbf{if } a > b \textbf{ then } a := a - b \textbf{ else } b := b - a \\
&\qquad \{GCD(a, b) = GCD(x, y)\} \\
&\qquad \{GCD(x, y) = a = b\} \\
&\textbf{end}
\end{aligned}$$
(7.19)

Note that with the aid of suitable indentation conventions, the structure of the algorithm becomes visibly apparent in the program. In particular, statements belonging to the same structural entity should be indented by the same amount, and by the same technique, the correspondence of opening and closing brackets should be made easily recognizable.

Programs (7.16) and (7.18) compute the same results but differ in the amount of *computational effort* needed to arrive at those results. A measure of this effort can be obtained by counting the number of necessary principal operations of each type. Program (7.16) requires two additions and two assignments for each repetition. If we denote the effort of an addition by a and the one for an assignment by z, then the total effort necessary for the multiplication according to (7.16) is

$$2z + 2(z + a) * x \tag{7.20}$$

For each repetition, program (7.18) requires one doubling, one halving, one test for even or odd, and either two or three assignments plus one addition. This separation of two cases makes an exact specification of the effort as a function of the operands rather difficult. It is easy, however, to indicate the worst and the best cases and, more importantly, to observe that due to the halving of u during each repetition, the maximum number of repetitions is $\log_2(x) + 1$ (rounded up). The total (worst case) effort then becomes

$$3z + \log_2(x) * (3z + a + 2h) \tag{7.21}$$

Since computers using a binary internal representation of numbers can execute multiplications and divisions by 2 and tests for even/odd very quickly (i.e., $h \leq a$), program (7.18) is superior to (7.16) even for small x. It is therefore preferred in all practical applications.

Program (7.22) represents an improvement over the division algorithm (7.17), which is based on the same principle. With the aid of the given invariants, the correctness of the improved algorithm can easily be established, and at the same time, the mode of operation becomes evident. q, r, and w are variables with natural numbers as values.

Program to divide the natural number *x* by *y*

$$
\begin{aligned}
&\textbf{begin } r := x; q := 0; w := y; \\
&\quad \textbf{while } w \leq r \textbf{ do } w := 2 * w; \\
&\quad \{w = 2^n * y > x\} \\
&\quad \textbf{while } w \neq y \textbf{ do} \\
&\quad \textbf{begin } \{q * w + r = x, r \geq 0\} \\
&\quad\quad q := 2 * q; w := w \textbf{ div } 2; \\
&\quad\quad \textbf{if } w \leq r \textbf{ then} \\
&\quad\quad\quad \textbf{begin } r := r - w; q := q + 1 \\
&\quad\quad\quad \textbf{end} \\
&\quad \textbf{end} \\
&\quad \{q * y + r = x, 0 \leq r < w; q = x \textbf{ div } y\} \\
&\textbf{end.}
\end{aligned}
$$

(7.22)

The reduction of computing effort is again due to the technique of devising a step that needs to be repeated only $\log_2(x/y) + 1$ instead of x/y times.

By replacing repeated subtractions by divisions, program (6.2), which computes the greatest common divisor, can also be modified into a more efficient version. To simplify the notation, we introduce the operator **mod,** yielding the remainder of the integer division with the same operands x and y; that is,

$$\underbrace{(x \text{ div } y)}_{\text{quotient}} * y + \underbrace{(x \text{ mod } y)}_{\text{remainder}} = x \qquad (7.23)$$

The repeated subtraction

$$\textbf{while } a \geq b \textbf{ do } a := a - b \qquad (7.24.1)$$

can then be replaced by the simple assignment

$$a := a \text{ mod } b \qquad (7.24.2)$$

Program (6.2) written in serial notation as indicated in (7.25), is thereby transformed into program (7.26).

```
begin a := x; b := y;
    repeat {a > 0, b > 0}
        while a > b do a := a − b;
        while b > a do b := b − a;          (7.25)
    until a = b
    {a = b = GCD(x, y)}
end.
```

```
begin a := x; b := y;
    repeat {a > 0, b > 0}
        if a ≧ b then a := a mod b;          (7.26)
        {0 ≦ a < b}
        if a > 0 then b := b mod a else Exchange(a, b)
    until b = 0
    {a = GCD(x, y)}
end.
```

This version of computing the greatest common divisor was invented by *Euclid* and is one of the earliest known examples of a mathematical algorithm. It is usually quoted in the equivalent form (7.27).

$$\begin{aligned}&\textbf{begin } a := x;\, b := y;\\&\quad\textbf{repeat } a := a \textbf{ mod } b;\, Exchange(a, b)\\&\quad\textbf{until } b = 0\\&\quad\{a = GCD(x, y)\}\\&\textbf{end.}\end{aligned}$$ (7.27)

Verification is easy using relation (7.28).

$$x > y: GCD(x, y) = GCD(x \textbf{ mod } y, y)$$ (7.28)

EXERCISES

7.1 Determine which of the following symbol sequences constitute numbers, constants, variables, factors, terms, expressions, or statements according to the syntax-diagrams given in Appendix A. Note the classification of operators into three sets with different priorities.

$$\begin{aligned}&\text{relational operators}\quad = \neq < \leqq \geqq >\\&\text{additive operators}\qquad + - \vee\\&\text{multiplicative operators}\qquad * / \textbf{ div mod } \wedge\end{aligned}$$

Numbers	0.31	+ 237.2	3.5	− 0.005
	4.555	3 + 5	3E5	two
	33,75	.389	1E00	15
	$10E - 4$	1.5 + 2	00037	3,250
Constants	100	*true*	+ 15.5	*red*
	$'A'$	*nine*	9/5	$'*'$
Variables	x	$A[i]$	$x + y$	$B[i, j]$
Factors	$B[i, j]$	$sin(x)$	p	$p \vee q$
	(x)	$x * y$	$x - y$	$exp(y * ln(x))$
Terms	(x)	$x * y$	$x - y$	$(x - y)$
Expressions	x	2	$a = b$	$+ x * y$
	(x)	$(x \leqq y) \wedge (y < z)$	$p < q \wedge r < s$	*true*
Statements				

$$\begin{aligned}&a := b \qquad a := 2 \qquad 2 := a \sin(x * y)\\&\textbf{begin } a := 1 \textbf{ end}\\&\textbf{if } a = 2 \textbf{ then } a := a + 1 \textbf{ else } P(x, y)\\&\textbf{while } a > 0 \textbf{ do } a := a - 1 \textbf{ end}\\&\textbf{if } x < y \textbf{ then}; z := true; \textbf{ else } z := false\\&\textbf{repeat } z := z + 1.5,\ y := u - 1 \textbf{ until } y = 0\end{aligned}$$

7.2 Evaluate the following expressions.

$$2 * 3 - 4 * 5 \; =$$
$$15 \text{ div } 4 * 4 \quad =$$
$$80/5/3 \qquad =$$
$$2/3 * 2 \qquad =$$

Then describe the following expressions in the language defined by the syntax in Appendix A.

$$a^2 - c + \cfrac{a}{b * c + \cfrac{c}{d + \cfrac{e}{f}}}$$

$$\frac{-b + \sqrt{b^2 - 4ac}}{2a}$$

$$\tfrac{1}{2} * \ln\left|\frac{w - a}{w + a}\right|$$

$$\frac{\dfrac{1}{a} + \dfrac{1}{b}}{c + d}$$

7.3 Execute the programs indicated with the specified values of x and y and establish a trace table.

(a) Programs (7.16) and (7.18):
     $(x, y) = (3, 5), (2, 11), (10, 8), (19, 2)$

(b) Programs (7.17) and (7.22):
     $(x, y) = (83, 15), (117, 9), (23, 27), (1191, 37)$

(c) Programs (7.19), (7.25), and (7.27):
     $(x, y) = (84, 36), (36, 84), (770, 441), (15, 15)$

7.4 Determine upper and lower bounds for the number of necessary operations (as functions of x and y) in program 7.22. Then determine the necessary and sufficient assertions for verification of the program.

7.5 Translate flow-diagram (7.29) into serial notation. Note that the program computes the greatest common divisor $GCD(x, y)$ and two multipliers c and d so that

$$c * x + d * y = GCD(x, y)$$

Determine the necessary and sufficient assertions for program verification.

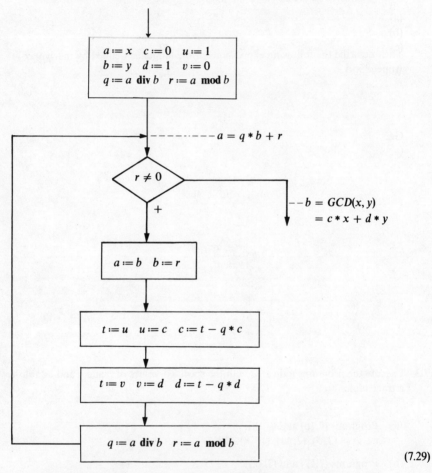

(7.29)

7.6 Construct a program, annotated with the necessary assertions for verification, that computes $GCD(x, y)$ only on the basis of the following relations.
(a) $GCD(2 * m, 2 * n) = 2 * GCD(m, n)$
(b) $odd(n): GCD(2 * m, n) = GCD(m, n)$
(c) $m > n: GCD(m - n, n) = GCD(m, n)$
(d) $GCD(n, m) = GCD(m, n)$
(e) $odd(m) \wedge odd(n): \neg odd(m - n)$

Use only subtraction, comparison, halving and doubling operations.

7.7 Among the conditions P, Q, and R, exactly one is satisfied at all times. (They are called mutually exclusive conditions.) The probability that P is satisfied is W_P. (W_Q and W_R are defined analogously.) Determine the expected value of necessary evaluations of P, Q, R as functions of W_P, W_Q, W_R in the following statements:

(a) **if** P **then** A **else if** Q **then** B **else** C
(b) **if** Q **then** B **else if** R **then** C **else** A
(c) **if** R **then** C **else if** P **then** A **else** B

Which of the three equivalent statements is selected if $W_P > W_Q > W_R$?

$$\text{Example:} \quad P = (x > y), \quad Q = (x = y), \quad R = (x < y);$$
$$W_P = 0.5, \quad W_Q = 0.3, \quad W_R = 0.2$$

Generalize the obtained rule to the case with n mutually exclusive conditions ($n > 3$).

8 DATA TYPES

In Chapter 5 we discussed how the explicit specification of all variables in the heading of a program—an essential part of its documentation–contributes significantly to the program's readability. The introduction of a new variable, in particular, should be accompanied by the specification of its range of possible values. There are several important reasons for these recommendations.

1. Knowledge of the range of values of variables is essential in understanding an algorithm. Without explicit specification, it is usually difficult to determine the kind of objects that a variable represents, thus making the discovery of programming mistakes more tedious.
2. In most cases, the suitability and the correctness of a program are dependent on the range of values of its arguments. Therefore the specification of value ranges is as much a part of program documentation as is an explanation of the results.
3. The number of storage units needed to represent a variable in a computer depends on the size of its value range. (For example, if the size of that range is n, then $\log_2(n)$ bits are needed.) To perform the necessary storage allocation, a compiler must know the variables' range of values.
4. Operators appearing in expressions are usually defined only for certain value ranges of their arguments. Using specified ranges of values, a compiler can check whether specified combinations of operators and operands are permissible, thereby detecting programming errors. In this respect, the indication of value ranges represents a redundancy that can be used to check certain properties of the program.
5. The implementation of operators often depends on the range of values of their permissible arguments. In such cases, knowledge of the range of values is absolutely necessary in obtaining an appropriate, efficient

representation of the program. The representation of numbers and the implementation of arithmetic operators is a typical example; the choice of machine instructions to execute an arithmetic operation usually depends on whether its arguments range over real numbers or only over integers.

The set of values that a variable may assume plays such an important role in the characterization of the variable that it is called its *type*. We therefore recommend that all variables be declared in the heading of a program. Such a *variable declaration* is denoted by

$$\textbf{var } v : T \tag{8.1}$$

where v is the identifier of the new variable and T is its type. If several variables of the same type are declared, the short form

$$\textbf{var } v_1, v_2, \ldots, v_m : T \tag{8.2}$$

where $v_1, \ldots, v_m$ are the declared variable identifiers, is applicable.

Declaring all identifiers in the heading of a program has the additional advantage of enabling a compiler to check whether each identifier in the program has been declared. If not (due to keypunch errors, misspellings, etc.), the compiler can make the programmer aware of this mistake—instead of introducing another variable with the misspelled name. Again, the redundancy of the program text is used to increase programming security.

Two questions now arise: how can a data type be appropriately introduced into a program, and how can data types be conveniently represented in computer stores? The first step is to distinguish certain classes of data types. The most important, single distinction is whether the values of a type are *structured*. If a value is *unstructured* (i.e., not decomposable into components), then it is called a *scalar*. In this chapter we will introduce only scalar types, deferring the notion of structured types to Chapters 10 and 11.

The general form of a *type definition is*

$$\textbf{type } t = T \tag{8.3}$$

where t is the newly introduced identifier and T is a description of that type. A scalar type is described by an enumeration of its components. The notation

$$\textbf{type } t = (w_1, w_2, \ldots, w_n) \tag{8.4}$$

is used for this purpose. Such a definition introduces the *type identifier*, t, as well as the n *constant identifiers*, $w_1, \ldots, w_n$. Examples of scalar type definitions are

type *color* = (*red, yellow, green, blue*)
type *suit* = (*diamond, heart, spade, club*)
type *form* = (*triangular, rectangular, circular*)
type *state* = (*solid, liquid, gaseous*)

Note that if variables are of a type whose explicit naming is superfluous, then the type may be left anonymous by combining the variable declaration (8.2) and the type definition (8.4) into

$$\textbf{var } v_1, v_2, \ldots, v_m: (w_1, w_2, \ldots, w_n) \tag{8.5}$$

In our programming notation, elements of sets of values will not only be distinct but also *ordered*. The following axioms are postulated for any scalar type, t, as defined by (8.4).

1. $w_i \neq w_j$ for $i \neq j$ (distinctness)
2. $w_i < w_j$ for $i < j$ (ordering)   (8.6)
3. Only $w_1, \ldots, w_n$ are values of type t.

The existence of ordering makes it both possible and desirable to introduce the successor and predecessor functions.

$$\begin{aligned} succ(w_i) &= w_{i+1} \quad \text{for } i = 1, \ldots, n-1 \\ pred(w_i) &= w_{i-1} \quad \text{for } i = 2, \ldots, n \end{aligned} \tag{8.7}$$

If a program requires the inclusion of several scalar type definitions, then we will adhere to the rule that each constant identifier be declared only once, thereby enabling us to uniquely infer from every constant identifier the type of value that it denotes. Combinations of type definitions of the kind

$$\begin{aligned} \textbf{type } warmcolor &= (red, yellow, green) \\ coldcolor &= (green, blue) \end{aligned} \tag{8.8}$$

should be avoided because they leave the type of some constants (in this case, the color *green*) ambiguously defined.*

Certain scalar types are used so frequently that both they and their operators are present in every computer system. These types, called *standard types*, need not be defined in a program because it is assumed that they are known by every processor. They include the logical truth values, the whole

---

* The notions of union and intersection of types have been avoided intentionally.

and the real numbers, and a set of (printable) characters. They are used so frequently that their constants (except for the logical values, see Section 8.1) are denoted not by identifiers but by syntactically distinct constructs. We will now discuss the four main standard types.

8.1 TYPE *BOOLEAN*

The type *Boolean* denotes the range of *logical values* that consists of the two elements, *true and false*. It is named after the originator of logical calculus, George Boole (1815–1864), and is defined as

$$\textbf{type } Boolean = (\textit{false, true}) \tag{8.9}$$

The following *standard operators* are defined on arguments of this type.

$\lor$ logical inclusive OR
$\land$ logical AND
$\neg$ logical NOT

Given Boolean arguments p and q, the values of the expressions $p \lor q$, $p \land q$, and $\neg p$ are defined in table (8.10).

p	q	$p \lor q$	$p \land q$	$\neg p$
false	*false*	*false*	*false*	*true*
true	*false*	*true*	*false*	*false*
false	*true*	*true*	*false*	*true*
true	*true*	*true*	*true*	*false*

(8.10)

From this table, we can derive relations (8.11)–(8.14). These relations are useful in many instances, particularly when a simpler but still equivalent form of a given expression is sought.

1. $p \lor q = q \lor p$
   $p \land q = q \land p$ Commutative laws   (8.11)

2. $(p \lor q) \lor r = p \lor (q \lor r)$
   $(p \land q) \land r = p \land (q \land r)$ Associative laws   (8.12)

3. $(p \land q) \lor r = (p \lor r) \land (q \lor r)$
   $(p \lor q) \land r = (p \land r) \lor (q \land r)$ Distributive laws   (8.13)

4. $\neg(p \lor q) = \neg p \land \neg q$
   $\neg(p \land q) = \neg p \lor \neg q$ de Morgan's laws   (8.14)

As defined, the operator $\vee$ has less priority than $\wedge$, which, in turn, has less priority than $\neg$. For example, $\neg p \vee q \wedge r$ is read as $(\neg p) \vee (q \wedge r)$.

All *relational operators* yield a result of type *Boolean*. The expression $x = y$, for example, has the value *true* if x equals y—otherwise, *false*. The common relational operators are $=, \neq, <, \leqq, \geqq, >$, but the last four are evidently applicable only to ordered (i.e., scalar) types. The following relationships hold among these operators.

$$
\begin{aligned}
x \neq y &\leftrightarrow \neg(x = y) \\
x \leqq y &\leftrightarrow (x < y) \vee (x = y) \\
x \geqq y &\leftrightarrow \neg(x < y) \\
x > y &\leftrightarrow \neg(x < y) \wedge \neg(x = y)
\end{aligned}
\tag{8.15}
$$

With the aid of the logical connectives $\wedge$, $\vee$, and $\neg$, the six relational operators may therefore be expressed in terms of $=$ and $<$ only.

8.2 TYPE *INTEGER*

This type represents the set of *whole numbers*. The following operators are defined and assumed to be available in a given programming system.

$+$	addition
$-$	subtraction
$*$	multiplication
div	integer division
mod	remainder of integer division

Every computer system specifies a certain subset of the whole numbers (i.e., those that lie within certain limits) so that they can be directly and efficiently processed by its arithmetic unit. Consequently, type *integer* denotes the set of numbers that is defined by a given computer. Of course, these limits will vary from one computer to another. More importantly, the ordinary arithmetic axioms cannot be applied in general to computer arithmetic. They do not hold in cases where the true result of an operation lies outside the given finite range of values. For instance, if a certain system specifies type *integer* as the set of whole numbers with absolute value $|x| \leqq max$ and if we denote the computer-implemented addition by $\oplus$, then

$$x \oplus y = x + y$$

holds only if $|x + y| \leqq max$. Consequently, the ordinary associative law of addition is not generally valid for computer addition.

$$(x \oplus y) \oplus z = x \oplus (y \oplus z)$$

is satisfied only if both $|x \oplus y| \leqq max$ and $|y \oplus z| \leqq max$. By substituting values and setting $max = 100$, we see that e.g.

$$60 \oplus (50 \oplus (-40)) = 60 \oplus 10 = 70$$

whereas the result of evaluating

$$(60 \oplus 50) \oplus (-40)$$

is not defined. At first glance this situation seems rather hopeless. But remember that the range of whole numbers on most computers is fairly large compared with the requirements of most problems, so the case of too large and therefore undefined results (called *overflow*) seldom occurs. Nevertheless, a minimal requirement for every computer system is to provide a warning signal that terminates the computation if an overflow occurs— continuation with meaningless results would hardly make sense. Aside from the phenomenon of overflow, however, all *operations on arguments of type integer are assumed to be exact.*

In many cases, certain variables will assume values only within a specific interval. This information should then be reflected in the definition of the variable's type by explicitly indicating the intended interval. Such a type, called a *subrange type*, is defined as

$$\textbf{type } t = min .. max \tag{8.16}$$

The constants *min* and *max* denote the limits of the interval or subrange. Subrange definitions often enhance considerably the perspicuity of programs. Of course, the type *integer* itself is a subrange; its limits are defined by the particular computer or compiler system being used.

8.3 TYPE *CHAR*

This type denotes a finite, ordered *set of characters*. Just as it defines a certain range of processable numbers, every computer system also defines a set of characters through which it communicates with the outside world. These characters are available on its input (readers) and output (printers) equipment. A standardization of character sets is highly desirable, (even indispensable, if various computer systems are to be connected for mutual communication, data transmission, remote data processing, etc.). Although complete coordination in the standardization of character sets seems to be an elusive goal, it has been commonly agreed that character sets to be used by computer systems will comprise the 26 Latin *letters*, the 10 decimal Arabic *digits*, and a certain number of *special characters* such as punctuation marks. In addition, a character set defined by the International Standards Organization (ISO) and its American variant ASCII (American Standard

Code for Information Interchange) have gained widespread acceptance and use.

The ASCII set consists of 128 characters. Since $128 = 2^7$, each character can be represented or encoded as a unique combination of 7 bits. The mapping of bit combinations onto the set of characters is called a *code*; hence the ASCII code is called a *seven-bit code* (see Appendix B).

The ASCII characters are classified as *printable characters* and *control characters*. The printable characters are further subdivided into capital letters, lowercase letters, digits, and special characters. A further distinction is made between the *full* and the *restricted ASCII sets*. The latter, which excludes lowercase letters, is used on many commercially available devices.

The meaning of the control characters is explained in Appendix B; their main significance lies in data transmission. Here we will mention only two: **cr** (carriage return) and **lf** (line feed). When data are transmitted to a printing terminal, these characters signal the printer mechanism to reposition at the beginning of a new line.

TABLE OF ASCII CHARACTERS

	0	1	2	3	4	5	6	7
0	nul	dle		0	@	P	`	p
1	soh	dc1	!	1	A	Q	a	q
2	stx	dc2	"	2	B	R	b	r
3	etx	dc3	#	3	C	S	c	s
4	eot	dc4	$	4	D	T	d	t
5	enq	nak	%	5	E	U	e	u
6	ack	syn	&	6	F	V	f	v
7	bel	etb	'	7	G	W	g	w
8	bs	can	(	8	H	X	h	x
9	ht	em	)	9	I	Y	i	y
10	lf	sub	*	:	J	Z	j	z
11	vt	esc	+	;	K	[	k	{
12	ff	fs	,	<	L	\	l	|
13	cr	qs	-	=	M	]	m	}
14	so	rs	.	>	N	^	n	¬
15	si	us	/	?	O	_	o	del

Two standard functions (which depend on the underlying character set) allow the mapping of character sets onto subsets of natural numbers and vice versa. These functions, called *transfer functions*, have the following definitions.

ord(c)   is the ordinal number of the character c in the ordered character set. (Using the ASCII table, $ord(c) = 16 * x + y$ if x and y denote the coordinates of the character c).

chr(i)   is the character value with the ordinal number i.

Consequently, the relations

$$chr(ord(c)) = c \quad \text{and} \quad ord(chr(i)) = i \tag{8.17}$$

hold, and the ordering of the character set is defined by

$$c_1 < c_2 \quad \leftrightarrow \quad ord(c_1) < ord(c_2) \tag{8.18}$$

To denote a constant of type *char*, it is customary to enclose the character in apostrophes (or quotation marks). For example, if a question mark is assigned to a variable c of type *char*, then this is expressed as

$$c := \,'?'$$

In the programs in subsequent chapters, we will make no reference to a specific character set. However, the programs will make sense and perform according to their specifications only if they are applied to character sets with the following minimal properties.

1. The character set must contain the letters *A–Z* and the digits 0–9.
2. The subsets of letters and digits must be ordered and coherent. That is, c is a letter only if $'A' \leq c$ and $c \leq 'Z'$, and c is a digit if and only if $'0' \leq c$ and $c \leq '9'$.
3. The character set must contain a blank (space), a line separator (denoted by **eol**—meaning end of line), and several other characters, such as commas and periods, which are not specified in detail.

8.4   TYPE *REAL*

The fact that computer-representable ranges of values are always finite sets has particularly stringent and noticeable consequences in the treatment of real numbers. In the case of integers, it was reasonable to postulate that arithmetic operations generate exact results in every circumstance (except in overflow situations), but this claim is impossible to make for arithmetic with real numbers. The reason is that every arbitrarily small interval on the axis of real numbers contains infinitely many values; the real axis forms a so-called *continuum*. In programming, therefore, the type *real* does not represent an infinite, uncountable set of real numbers; instead, it is a *finite set of representatives of intervals* on the real continuum. The effects of performing computations with approximate instead of exact values depend largely on the problem to be solved and the algorithm that has been chosen. At best, the computed results will be approximations, with an inherent error, of the true results. The estimation (a very difficult task) of such errors, which are caused by the replacement of the real continuum by a finite set of representatives, is the subject of *Numerical Mathematics*. Computations on data of type *real* are called *numeric processes*. In a sense, "numeric" is synonymous with "inexact," without any derogative connotations.

But it is senseless to make computations without having some knowledge about the nature and the degree of imprecision to be expected. To comprehend and even to derive such measures, it is necessary to know the kind of representation used for real numbers with a finite number of digits. In modern digital computers, it has become customary to use the so-called *floating-point representation* in which a real number, x, is expressed by two integers, e and m, each with a finite number of digits, so that

$$x = m * B^e \qquad -E < e < E \qquad -M < m < M \qquad (8.19)$$

In this statement, m is called the *coefficient* (or *mantissa*); e is called the *exponent*; and B, E, M are constants that are characteristic of the representation. B is called the *base* of the floating-point representation and is usually not 10, but a small power of 2. A given value, x, can be denoted by many pairs $\langle m, e \rangle$. A canonical or *normalized form* is defined by the additional relation

$$\frac{M}{B} \leq m < M \qquad (8.20)$$

If the normalized form is used exclusively, then the density of representatives of intervals on the real-number axis decreases roughly exponentially with increasing $|x|$. The interval $[0.1 : 1]$, for instance, contains roughly as many representatives as does the interval $[10000 : 100000]$—and exactly as many if $B = 10$. The precise influence of this unequal distribution of representatives is difficult to determine for a given program, let alone in general. The elementary operations on arguments of type *real* are therefore defined not in exact terms, but in the form of minimal conditions, which must always be satisfied independently of the underlying specific floating-point arithmetic. These conditions can be stated in the form of axioms.

A1. Type *real* (denoted by R) is a *finite* subset of the set R of real numbers.

$$R \subset \mathbf{R}$$

A2. Every number $x \in R$ is associated with a number $\tilde{x} \in R$ called the *representative of x*.

A3. Every $\tilde{x} \in R$ represents many $x \in R$, but the set of represented values is a coherent interval on the real-number axis. That is, if $x_1 < x_2$, $\tilde{x}_1 = r$ and $\tilde{x}_2 = r$, then $\tilde{x} = r$ for all $x_1 \leq x \leq x_2$. Furthermore,

$$x \in R \quad \text{implies} \quad \tilde{x} = x$$

In particular, 0 and 1 are represented exactly. That is, $0 \in R$ and $1 \in R$; therefore $\tilde{0} = 0$ and $\tilde{1} = 1$.

A4. There exists a value, *max*, such that the representatives of all x with $|x| \geq max$ are undefined. The range of numbers $|x| \geq max$ is called the *overflow range* U. $R - U$ is coherent.

From Axioms A1–A4 it follows that

$$
\begin{aligned}
x < y \quad &\text{implies} \quad \tilde{x} \leq \tilde{y} \\
x = y \quad &\text{implies} \quad \tilde{x} = \tilde{y} \\
x > y \quad &\text{implies} \quad \tilde{x} \geq \tilde{y}
\end{aligned}
\tag{8.21}
$$

A5. R is symmetric with respect to 0; that is,

$$(-x)^{\sim} = -(\tilde{x}) \tag{8.22}$$

Axioms A6–A9 postulate a set of minimal properties that must be fulfilled by a computer's arithmetic before it can be called "usable" without reservations. The basic arithmetic operations discussed are addition, subtraction, multiplication, and division, denoted by the symbols $\oplus$, $\ominus$, $\otimes$ and $\oslash$, respectively. We will always assume $x, y \in R$.

A6. *Commutativity* of addition and multiplication

$$x \oplus y = y \oplus x, \qquad x \otimes y = y \otimes x \tag{8.23}$$

A7. $$x \geq y \geq 0 \to (x \ominus y) \oplus y = x \tag{8.24}$$

A8. *Symmetry* of the basic operations with respect to 0

$$
\begin{aligned}
x \ominus y &= x \oplus (-y) = -(y \ominus x) \\
(-x) \otimes y &= x \otimes (-y) = -(x \otimes y) \\
(-x) \oslash y &= x \oslash (-y) = -(x \oslash y)
\end{aligned}
\tag{8.25}
$$

A9. *Monotonicity* of the basic operations

$$0 \leq x \leq a \quad \text{and} \quad 0 \leq y \leq b$$

implies

$$
\begin{aligned}
x \oplus y &\leq a \oplus b & x \ominus b &\leq a \ominus y \\
x \otimes y &\leq a \otimes b & x \oslash b &\leq a \oslash y
\end{aligned}
\tag{8.26}
$$

As a consequence of A9, it is entirely possible that for certain x and y such that $0 \leqq x < a$ and $0 \leqq y < b$,

$$x \oplus y = a \oplus b \quad \text{or} \quad x \otimes y = a \otimes b$$

but it is impossible that

$$x \oplus y > a \oplus b \quad \text{or} \quad x \otimes y > a \otimes b$$

From Axioms A1–A9, the following theorems, representing important basic properties of an arithmetic, may be derived.

$$
\begin{aligned}
y \geqq 0 &\rightarrow x \oplus y \geqq x \\
x \geqq y &\rightarrow x \ominus y \geqq 0 \\
(x \geqq 0) \wedge (0 \leqq y \leqq 1) &\rightarrow x \otimes y \leqq x \\
0 < x \leqq y &\rightarrow x \oslash y \leqq 1
\end{aligned}
\tag{8.27}
$$

$$x \ominus x = 0$$
$$x \oplus 0 = x \ominus 0 = x$$
$$x \otimes 0 = 0$$
$$x \otimes 1 = x \oslash 1 = x$$
$$x \oslash x = 1$$

Note that the ordinary *associative and distributive laws* of arithmetic are conspicuously absent from axioms A1–A9. There are good reasons for this omission. First, look at this numeric example, which violates the associative law of addition. It is based on a number representation with four decimal digits. (The exponent e is implied in the position of the decimal point.)

$$x = 9.900 \quad y = 1.000 \quad z = -0.999$$

1. $(x \oplus y) \oplus z = 10.90 \oplus (-0.999) = 9.910$
2. $x \oplus (y \oplus z) = 9.900 \oplus 0.001 = 9.901$

Then look at this numeric example (also based on a four-digit decimal arithmetic), which violates the distributive law.

$$x = 1100. \quad y = -5.000 \quad z = 5.001$$

1. $(x \otimes y) \oplus (x \otimes z) = -5500. \oplus 5501. = 1.000$
2. $x \otimes (y \oplus z) = 1100. \otimes 0.001 = 1.100$

The "dangerous" operations are addition and subtraction. They give rise to significant errors, particularly if two almost equal values are subtracted. In that case, the most significant digits cancel themselves, and the resulting difference loses a number or possibly all of the significant digits. This phenomenon is called *cancellation*.

But the division operation also represents a potential source of pitfalls. In the case of small divisors, the result may easily fall within the overflow range. Therefore, division by zero and division by values "close" to zero should always be avoided. For instance, a relation of the form $abs(t/x) \leqq eps$ should not be used in a program; instead it should be replaced by the division-free form $abs(t) \leqq eps * abs(x)$.

A measure of the *precision* of a given floating-point arithmetic is found in the quantity ε, which is defined as follows:

$$\varepsilon = \min_{x>0} (x \mid (1 + x)^{\sim} \neq 1) \qquad (8.28)$$

That is, ε is the least positive number such that the representatives of 1 and $1 + \varepsilon$ differ. If, for example, a computer represents real numbers by n decimal digits, its ε is approximately 10^{-n}.

Although in the mathematical sense the integers are a subset of the real numbers, it is customary and appropriate to consider the types *integer* and *real* as disjoint. To satisfy the notational ground rule that the type of a constant should be apparent from its denotation, we will assume that a number is of type *integer* if and only if its denotation contains neither a decimal point nor a scale factor (see Chapter 7). All numbers denoted with either a decimal point or a scale factor are assumed to be of type *real*. In programming with *real* objects, we have adopted the following, additional conventions.

1. In a real-valued expression, any real-valued operand may be replaced by an integer-valued operand. An explicit transfer function from type integer to type real is therefore unnecessary. Nevertheless, the programmer must be aware of the fact that a compiler has to automatically insert *implicit conversion instructions* at every such occurrence, if the computer uses different internal representations for values of the two types (most computers do).

2. If a real-valued argument is used where only an integer is legal, then an explicit transfer function must be indicated. As a standard transfer function, we have adopted the one whose realization is most straightforward on existing computers, namely,

$$trunc(x)$$

which represents the integer obtained by truncating the fractional part of x. Examples are

$$trunc\ (5.8) = 5, \qquad trunc\ (4.3) = 4$$

The rounding function is now expressible as

$$round\ (x) = \begin{cases} trunc\ (x + 0.5) & \text{for } x \geqq 0 \\ -trunc\ (0.5 - x) & \text{for } x < 0 \end{cases}$$

Example: Solving a quadratic equation

This example will help to make programmers aware of the kinds of pitfalls they may encounter when dealing with *real* arithmetic and to demonstrate how these pitfalls can be overcome.

The problem consists of computing the two solutions, x_1 and x_2, of the quadratic equation

$$a * x^2 + b * x + c = 0 \qquad a \neq 0 \tag{8.29.1}$$

A literal translation of the well-known formula

$$x_{1,2} = \frac{-b \pm \sqrt{b^2 - 4ac}}{2a} \tag{8.29.2}$$

yields the following program statements.

$$d := sqrt(sqr(b) - 4 * a * c);$$
$$x_2 := -(b + d)/(2 * a); \quad x_1 := (d - b)/(2 * a)$$

A numeric example with the values $a = 1.000$, $b = -200.0$, and $c = 1.000$, executed with a four-digit decimal arithmetic, yields

$$d = sqrt(40000 - 4.000) = 200.0$$
$$x_1 = 400.0/2.000 = 200.0 \tag{8.30}$$
$$x_2 = 0.000/2.000 = 0.000$$

The correct results, however, are $x_1 = 200.0$ and $x_2 = 0.005$. If our measuring scale for the quality of this program is based on relative accuracy, then the result x_2 must be rejected as being completely wrong.

An algorithm that takes into account the pitfalls of using a floating-point arithmetic with finite accuracy is based on the relation

$$x_1 * x_2 = c/a \quad \text{(Vieta)} \tag{8.31}$$

Using (8.29.2), we now compute only one solution—the one with the larger absolute value. The second solution is then obtained, according to (8.31), by using only multiplication and division—operations that preserve the arguments' relative accuracy. The resulting program statements are

$$d := sqrt(sqr(b) - 4 * a * c);$$
$$\textbf{if } b \geq 0 \textbf{ then } x1 := -(b + d)/(2 * a) \tag{8.32}$$
$$\qquad \textbf{else } x1 := (d - b)/(2 * a);$$
$$x2 := c/(x1 * a)$$

This problem is an example of the relatively frequent case in which the commonly taught mathematical methods of solution cannot be adopted without further examination and scrutiny, if the solutions are to be obtained with the aid of a computer.

EXERCISES

8.1 Which of the following expressions are syntactically correct (i.e., "type compatible")? What are their types? Assume that the following variables are declared.

var x, y, z: *real*; i, j, k: *integer*

$x + y * i$	$i \bmod (j + y)$	$i + j - k$
$i \dim j + x$	$x + y < i + j$	$k - \text{trunc}(x * i)$
$i * x + j * y$	$x < y \land y < z$	$x = i$

Indicate in each case the number of necessary, implicit integer-to-real transfer operations.

8.2 Complete programs (7.16), (7.17), (7.18), (7.19), (7.22), and (7.25) by adding the necessary variable declarations.

8.3 Design a program that computes the sum

$$1 - 1/2 + 1/3 - 1/4 + \cdots + 1/9999 - 1/10000$$

in the following ways:
(a) addition of terms from left to right,
(b) addition of terms from right to left,
(c) separate addition of positive and negative terms, each from left to right,
(d) separate addition of positive and negative terms, each from right to left.
Try to develop several programs to compute the four sums and weigh their respective advantages and disadvantages. Compare the four results obtained by using a computer and explain their differences.
Hint: Statements of the form $a := b * (-1)$ should be expressed instead as $a := -b$. The sum with 30-digit accuracy is

$$0.69309718305994529691723237145 8$$

8.4 Design a program that repeatedly multiplies the complex variable z by the complex constant $c = 0.6 + 0.8i$. A complex number $z = x + iy$ ($i = \sqrt{-1}$) should be represented by two real-valued variables, x and y.
Note: The absolute value of c is 1. If the program includes a computation of

$$|z| = \text{sqrt}(x^2 + y^2)$$

then the difference between the final and the initial values of $|z|$ may be used as a measure of the precision of the computer's floating-point arithmetic. Choose $n = 500$ and an initial value $|z| = 1$.

8.5 Show that for every floating-point arithmetic with finite precision and base $B > 2$, there exist numbers x such that

$$(x \oplus x)/2 \neq x$$

Hint: First find such an x by using a two-digit decimal representation.

9 PROGRAMS BASED ON RECURRENCE RELATIONS

9.1 SEQUENCES

Having introduced some fundamental program structures and basic data types in the previous chapters, we will now investigate in detail programs that consist essentially of *one repeated statement*, that is, those of the general form

$$\textbf{while } B \textbf{ do } S \tag{9.1}$$

where B is a Boolean expression and S is a statement. First, we observe that the repetition will terminate only if statement S influences B in such a way that after a finite number of executions of S, expression B becomes false. But this implies that there must be at least one assignment within S to a variable that occurs in B. If we introduce V as denoting the entire set of variables occurring in the program—thus considering each variable as a component of V—then statement (9.1) can be represented in the general form (9.2), which is an example of a so-called *program schema*.

$$
\boxed{
\begin{aligned}
&V := v_0; \\
&\textbf{while } p(V) \textbf{ do } V := f(V)
\end{aligned}
} \tag{9.2}
$$

Here p denotes a condition (Boolean expression) and f a function. (9.2) is called a schema because by suitable substitutions of V, p, and f, many different concrete programs can be constructed, all having identical underlying structures and patterns of behavior.

If we denote the value of the variable V after the ith execution of S by v_i, then V successively assumes the sequence of values

$$v_0, v_1, \ldots, v_n \tag{9.3}$$

58

which have the following properties.

1. $v_i = f(v_{i-1})$ for all $i > 0$
2. $v_i \neq v_j$ for all $i \neq j$
3. $\neg p(v_n)$
4. $p(v_i)$ for all $i < n$

$$(9.4)$$

Rule 1 follows from the definition of assignment (7.9), rule 2 from the considerations above, and rules 3 and 4 from the definition of the **while** statement in (7.13). Note that V must have a well-defined *initial value* v_0; the failure to observe this fundamental rule is one of the most frequent programming errors. The iteration terminates, if there exists an n such that condition 3 is satisfied.

The lesson to be learned is that the statement with the **while** clause is the appropriate form in which to express programs whose purpose and aim is specified by a *recurrence relation* (9.4.1.).

Example: Computation of factorials
The function

$$f(n) = n! = 1 * 2 * \cdots * n \qquad n \geq 0 \qquad (9.5)$$

can be computed according to a program derived from schema (9.2) by using the recurrence relations

$$f(i) = i * f(i - 1)$$
$$f(0) = 1 \qquad\qquad (9.6)$$

In the program, we introduce two variables F and K whose values after the ith execution of the repeated statement are $f(i)$ and i, respectively; that is, their recurrence relations are

$$\left.\begin{array}{l} f_i = k_i * f_{i-1} \\ k_i = k_{i-1} + 1 \end{array}\right\} \quad \text{for } i > 0 \qquad (9.7)$$

and their initial values are

$$f_0 = 1, \qquad k_0 = 0$$

The program derived by substituting recurrence relations (9.7) in schema (9.2) is

```
var F, K : integer ; {n ≥ 0}
begin F := 1 ; K := 0 ;
    while K ≠ n do
    begin {F = K!}
        K := K + 1 ; F := K * F
    end
    {F = n!}
end
```

$$(9.8)$$

Since K progresses through the sequence of natural numbers and since $n \geq 0$, the program terminates. It is particularly noteworthy that the order in which the two repeated statements are executed is relevant. If they were interchanged to

$$F := K * F; \quad K := K + 1 \qquad (9.9.1)$$

then the corresponding recurrence relations would be

$$f_i = k_{i-1} * f_{i-1} \qquad (9.9.2)$$

$$k_i = k_{i-1} + 1$$

which differ slightly but significantly from (9.7).

Example: Computation of 1/x

Let two sequences of real numbers $a_0, a_1, \ldots$ and $c_0, c_1, \ldots$ be specified by the recurrence relations

$$\left. \begin{array}{l} a_i = a_{i-1} * (1 + c_{i-1}) \\ c_i = c_{i-1}^2 \end{array} \right\} \quad \text{for } i > 0 \qquad (9.10)$$

and the initial values

$$a_0 = 1, \qquad c_0 = 1 - x \qquad 0 < x < 1$$

By algebraic manipulation of formulas, it can be shown that

$$a_n = \frac{1 - c_n}{x} \qquad (9.11)$$

and since $c_n = c_0^{2^n}$ and $|c_0| < 1$, it follows that

$$\lim_{n \to \infty} a_n = \frac{1}{x} \qquad (9.12)$$

Hint: To derive (9.11) from (9.10), use the relations

$$a_n = (1 + c_{n-1}) * \cdots * (1 + c_1) * (1 + c_0)$$

$$\frac{1 + c_{i-1}}{1 - c_i} = \frac{1}{1 - c_{i-1}}$$

By substituting recurrence relations (9.10) in schema (9.2), we obtain program (9.13), which computes an *approximation* of $1/x$ by using additions and multiplications only.

```
var A, C: real; {0 < x < 1}
begin A := 1; C := 1 - x;
    while abs(C) > ε do
        begin {A * x = 1 - C, 0 < C < 1}          (9.13)
            A := A * (1 + C); C := sqr(C)
        end
    {(1 - ε)/x ≤ A < 1/x}
end.
```

Program (9.13) terminates when C reaches a value $c_n \leqq \varepsilon$. Since $|c_0| < 1$ (cf. 9.10) and $c_n = c_0^{2^n}$, the existence of a value n such that $c_n \leqq \varepsilon$ is guaranteed for arbitrarily small ε. For all $i < n$, however, $c_i > \varepsilon$ (cf. 9.4).

Example: Computation of square roots

Let the two sequences of real numbers $a_0, a_1, \ldots$ and $c_0, c_1, \ldots$ be given by the recurrence relations

$$\left. \begin{array}{l} a_i = a_{i-1} * (1 + \tfrac{1}{2} c_{i-1}) \\ c_i = c_{i-1}^2 * \tfrac{1}{4}(3 + c_{i-1}) \end{array} \right\} \text{ for } i > 0 \qquad (9.14)$$

and the initial values

$$a_0 = x, \qquad c_0 = 1 - x \qquad 0 < x < 1$$

By suitable manipulation of formulas, it can be shown that

$$a_n = \sqrt{x * (1 - c_n)} \qquad (9.15)$$

Since $|c_0| > 0$,

$$\lim_{n \to \infty} c_n = 0 \quad \text{and} \quad \lim_{n \to \infty} a_n = \sqrt{x} \qquad (9.16)$$

Hint: To derive (9.15) from (9.14), use the relations

$$a_n = (1 + \tfrac{1}{2} c_{n-1}) * (1 + \tfrac{1}{2} c_{n-2}) * \cdots * (1 + \tfrac{1}{2} c_0) * x$$

$$(1 + \tfrac{1}{2} c_{i-1}) = \frac{\sqrt{1 - c_i}}{\sqrt{1 - c_{i-1}}}$$

and

$$\frac{x}{a_n} = \frac{1}{(1 + \tfrac{1}{2} c_0) \cdots (1 + \tfrac{1}{2} c_{n-1})} = \frac{\sqrt{1 - c_{n-1}}}{(1 + \tfrac{1}{2} c_0) \cdots (1 + \tfrac{1}{2} c_{n-2}) \sqrt{1 - c_n}} = \cdots$$

$$= \frac{\sqrt{1 - c_1}}{(1 + \tfrac{1}{2} c_0) \sqrt{1 - c_n}} = \frac{\sqrt{1 - c_0}}{\sqrt{1 - c_n}} = \frac{\sqrt{x}}{\sqrt{1 - c_n}}$$

The program obtained by substituting recurrence relations (9.14) in program schema (9.2) is

```
var A, C: real; {0 < x < 1}                          (9.17)
begin A := x; C := 1 − x;
    while abs(C) > ε do
       begin {A² = x * (1 − C), C ≥ 0}
          A := A * (1 + 0.5 * C);
          C := sqr(C) * (0.75 + 0.25 * C)
       end
    {x * (1 − ε) ≤ A² < x}
end.
```

The program terminates because of relation (9.16.1), which guarantees the existence of an n such that $c_n \leqq \varepsilon$ for arbitrarily small ε.

9.2 SERIES

The basic repetitive form of a statement is suitable to compute not only sequences but also *series* of numbers. Given the sequence of terms

$$t_0, t_1, t_2, \ldots \tag{9.18}$$

the series of partial sums

$$s_0, s_1, s_2, \ldots \tag{9.19}$$

is defined such that

$$s_i = t_0 + t_1 + \cdots + t_i \tag{9.20}$$

If the sequence is given by the recurrence relation

$$t_i = f(t_{i-1}) \quad \text{for } i > 0 \tag{9.21}$$

then the series is determined by

$$s_i = s_{i-1} + t_i \quad \text{for } i > 0$$
$$s_0 = t_0 \tag{9.22}$$

Figure (9.23) shows the program schema that—after suitable substitutions of f and t_0—yields programs that will assign to the variable S the value s_i in the ith repetition.

$$
\boxed{
\begin{aligned}
&T := t_0; \, S := T; \\
&\textbf{while } p(S, T) \textbf{ do} \\
&\textbf{begin } T := f(T); \, S := S + T \\
&\textbf{end}
\end{aligned}
}
\tag{9.23}
$$

From the definition of the assignment statement and the repeated statement using the **while** clause, the following relations can be derived as the basic properties of this program schema.

$$
\begin{array}{lll}
1. & t_i = f(t_{i-1}) & \text{for } i > 0 \\
2. & t_i \neq t_j & \text{for } i \neq j \\
3. & s_i = s_{i-1} + t_i & \text{for } i > 0 \\
4. & \neg p(s_n, t_n) & \\
5. & p(s_i, t_i) & \text{for all } i < n
\end{array}
\tag{9.24}
$$

Example: Approximation of exp (x)
The terms of the sums

$$s_i = 1 + x + \frac{x^2}{2!} + \cdots + \frac{x^i}{i!} \qquad (9.25)$$

are defined by the recurrence relation

$$t_j = t_{j-1} * x/j \qquad j > 0 \qquad (9.26)$$

and the initial value $t_0 = 1$. The limit of the series is known to be

$$\lim_{n \to \infty} s_n = exp(x) \qquad (9.27)$$

The series converges to a limit for all real numbers x; that is, the terms decrease such that their sum converges to a fixed limit. This fact is used by program (9.28), which was obtained by substituting recurrence relation (9.26) in program schema (9.23).

```
var T, S: real; K: integer;
begin T := 1; S := T; K := 0;                          (9.28)
      while T > ε do
        begin {S = 1 + x + ... + x^K/K!,  T = x^K/K! > ε}
               K := K + 1;  T := T * x/K;  S := S + T
        end
end.
```

The "error" by which the final value of S differs from the true limit sum is $\sum_{i=K+1}^{\infty} (x^i/i!)$ which can be made arbitrarily small by choosing K sufficiently large. It is customary to terminate the summation depending on the magnitude of terms *relative* to the total sum rather than the absolute value of the last term. This strategy requires, however, a further analysis of the convergence of the series, particularly if its terms have alternating signs. The following is an example of such a case.

Example: Approximation of sin (x)
The components of the series s

$$s_i = x - \frac{x^3}{3!} + \frac{x^5}{5!} - \cdots + (-1)^{2i-1} * \frac{x^{2i-1}}{(2^i - 1)!} \qquad (9.29)$$

consist of terms defined by the recurrence relations

$$t_j = -t_{j-1} * \frac{x^2}{k_j * (k_j - 1)} \qquad (9.30)$$

$$k_j = k_{j-1} + 2$$

for $j > 0$ and the initial values $t_0 = x$ and $k_0 = 1$. The limit of s is known to be

$$\lim_{n \to \infty} s_n = sin(x) \tag{9.31}$$

The program resulting from the substitution of recurrence relations (9.30) in schema (9.23) is

```
var S, T: real; K: integer;
begin T := x; K := 1; S := T;
    while abs(T) > ε * abs(S) do                          (9.32)
    begin K := K + 2;  T := -T * sqr(x)/(K * (K - 1));
        S := S + T
    end
end.
```

It is particularly noteworthy that in programs (9.13), (9.17), (9.28), and (9.32), the number of necessary terms and the number of repetitions of computations are not easily determined. They depend on the value ε, the tolerated error in the termination condition, and also on the *rate of convergence* of the series. The use of such recurrence relations in programming therefore requires great care—even if mathematical analysis guarantees (ultimate) convergence—because fast convergence is highly desirable for practical purposes (cf. Exercises 9.3 and 9.8).

In (9.25) the rate of convergence is high only for small positive values of x. Consequently, we recommend using relations

$$exp(-x) = 1/exp(x) \quad \text{for } x < 0 \tag{9.33.1}$$

and

$$exp(i + y) = exp(i) * exp(y) \quad \text{for } x > 1 \tag{9.33.2}$$

whereby $i = trunc(x)$ and $y = x - i$. The value $exp(i)$ is then computed simply by repeated multiplication of the basis of the natural logarithms.

The terms in (9.29) have *alternating signs*, and the sum converges fast only for small values of x. The use of the following relations is therefore recommended for larger values of x.

$$sin(x) = sin(x - 2\pi n) \quad \text{for } 2\pi n \leqq |x| < 2\pi(n + 1)$$

$$sin(x) = -sin(x - \pi) \quad \text{for } \pi \leqq |x| < 2\pi$$

$$sin(x) = sin(\pi - x) \qquad \text{for } \frac{\pi}{2} \leqq |x| < \pi \tag{9.34}$$

$$sin(x) = cos\left(\frac{\pi}{2} - x\right) \quad \text{for } \frac{\pi}{4} < |x| < \frac{\pi}{2}$$

$$sin(x) = -sin(-x) \qquad \text{for } x < 0$$

By suitable application of these formulas, program (9.32) will have to be applied only to values of x satisfying $0 \leq |x| \leq \pi/4$. In this interval, however, the rate of convergence is satisfactory for practical purposes, and the number of terms to be computed remains sufficiently small to keep the effects of rounding and truncation errors (due to computation with a finite arithmetic) within tolerable limits.

Finally, program (9.32) calls for the application of another basic rule of programming: within the repeated statement, the value x^2 must be computed. This squaring is performed repeatedly, although x is never changed at all. This unnecessary computational effort can and must be eliminated by computing x^2 once—that is, before starting the repetitions in the **while** statement—and by assigning the result to an auxiliary variable, which is then substituted systematically for every occurrence of x^2. This procedure can be formulated as the following ground rule.

If an expression $f(x)$ is evaluated within a repetitive statement S and if the argument x does not change during the repetitions, then an auxiliary variable h must be introduced to which the value $f(x)$ is assigned once before the execution of S and which is substituted for every occurrence of $f(x)$ within S; that is, the construct

$$\textbf{while } P \textbf{ do}$$
$$\textbf{begin} \dots f(x) \dots \textbf{end} \qquad\qquad (9.35.1)$$

is replaced by

$$h := f(x);$$
$$\textbf{while } P \textbf{ do}$$
$$\textbf{begin} \dots h \dots \textbf{end} \qquad\qquad (9.35.2)$$

EXERCISES

9.1 Rewrite programs (9.28) and (9.32)—using formulas (9.33) and (9.34)—so that the functions *exp* (x) and *sin* (x) are computed efficiently (and more accurately).

9.2 Design a program to compute an approximation of *cos* (x) with a relative accuracy ε. Use program schema (9.23) and

$$cos\,(x) = 1 - \frac{x^2}{2!} + \frac{x^4}{4!} - \cdots$$

9.3 Use program schema (9.23) to develop a program to compute an approximation to the integral

$$\int_0^x exp(-u^2)\,du \;=\; x - \frac{x^3}{3*1!} + \frac{x^5}{5*2!} - \frac{x^7}{7*3!} + \cdots$$

Hint: Observe that the rate of convergence is low for $x > 1$. What are the consequences of the use of a computer with finite precision and a finite range of values? (For example, trace the terms computed for the cases $x = 1, 2, 3 \ldots$).

9.4   Construct a program according to schema (9.2) to compute the Fibonacci numbers by two different methods:

(a) according to the recurrence relation

$$f_{i+1} = f_i + f_{i-1} \qquad i > 0$$
$$f_0 = 0, \qquad f_1 = 1$$

(b) using the formula

$$f_i = round\,(c^i/\sqrt{5})$$

where $c = (1 + \sqrt{5})/2$.

In place of $\sqrt{5}$ use the approximate value 2.236068 and determine the least i for which the two computed values of f_i differ.

9.5   Verify the results in programs (9.13) and (9.17) by finding the necessary and sufficient assertions after each statement derived from the indicated invariants.

9.6   Design a program based on schema (9.2) to compute the logarithm to the base 2 of a real number. Use the relations

$$log\,(x) = -log\,(1/x) \qquad \text{for } 0 < x < 1$$
$$log\,(x) = n + log\,(x/2^n) \quad \text{for } x > 2^n$$

For $1 \le x < 2$, use the recurrence relations

$$a_i = \begin{cases} a_{i-1}^2 & \text{if } a_{i-1}^2 < 2 \\ \tfrac{1}{2}a_{i-1}^2 & \text{if } a_{i-1}^2 \ge 2 \end{cases}$$

$$b_1 = \tfrac{1}{2}b_{i-1}$$

$$s_i = \begin{cases} s_{i-1} & \text{if } a_{i-1}^2 < 2 \\ s_{i-1} + b_i & \text{if } a_{i-1}^2 \ge 2 \end{cases}$$

for $i > 0$, and $a_0 = x$, $b_0 = 1$, $s_0 = 0$. The computation should be terminated with $b_n \le \varepsilon$ for a given sufficiently small ε. Find the invariant of the repetition, verify the result

$$\lim_{n \to \infty} s_n = log\,(x)$$

and establish that the algorithm will terminate.

9.7   Investigate the consequences of replacing the small quantity ε by zero in programs (9.13), (9.17), and of replacing the termination condition in (9.28) and (9.32) by $s = s + t$. Do the resulting programs still terminate, if the use of a floating-point arithmetic with finite precision is assumed?

9.8 Execute programs (9.13), (9.17), (9.28), and (9.32) on a computer and augment them by introducing a counter for the number of repetitions performed. Determine experimentally the rate of convergence of these programs for various values of their argument x.

9.9 The following program was designed to compute the sum s of the first n terms of the sine series (9.29) for arguments x such that $0 \leq x \leq \pi/4$. Is the program correct? What should be criticized about it?

```
var i, v: integer; h, u, s: real;
begin i := 0; u := x; v := 1;
    h := sqr(x); s := u;
    repeat i := i + 2; u := -u * h;
        v := v * i * (i + 1); s := s + u/v
    until i > 2 * n
end.
```

9.10 Given a computer capable of representing real numbers with a relative accuracy $\varepsilon = 10^{-6}$ (10^{-10}, 10^{-14}), determine how many terms of the series (9.25) and (9.29) are necessary—in the worst case— to obtain the maximum possible accuracy of $exp(x)$ for $0 \leq x < 1$ and $sin(x)$ for $0 \leq x < \pi/4$ (cf. 8.28).

10 THE FILE DATA STRUCTURE

10.1 THE NOTION OF A FILE

The two most characteristic properties of the data types discussed so far are the indivisibility of their values and the existence of an ordering among them. Hence they are called scalar. For example, every value of type *integer* (i.e., every whole number) is a unit or an entity without components, and the set of integers is ordered. Thus it does not make sense to refer to the ith digit (component) of an integer, but it is sensible to talk about the ith digit of a decimal representation of an integer that itself is not an integer but a sequence of characters. In this case, therefore, it is obviously convenient to be able to refer to the representation of the number as a whole, although it consists of individual digits. This ability to give a collective name to an entire set of elements is of great value in data processing in general. Such sets of values or variables with a single collective name are said to be *structured*. There exist several methods of structuring, each distinguished by the manner in which individual components are accessible and therefore also by their denotation.

Variables consisting of several components are called *structured variables*. To define the type (range of values) of a structured variable, it is necessary to specify

(a) its structuring method, and
(b) the type(s) of its components.

In many ways, the simplest structuring method is the *sequence*. Perhaps the best known example of a variable with a sequence structure is the *card deck*. In the data processing profession, *sequential file* is the generally accepted term used to describe a sequence. Here we will simply use the word *file*, allowing the attribute "sequential" to be implied. To define a type F, that is, a range of values which are sequences of components of type T, we use the notation

$$\textbf{type } F = \textbf{file of } T \tag{10.1}$$

All components of the sequences are thereby defined to be of the *same* type T.

Example:

$$\textbf{type } text = \textbf{file of } char$$

Such a—notably infinite—range of values can be defined formally with the aid of the operation of concatenation: the *concatenation* of two files

$$\alpha = \langle x_1, x_2 \ldots x_m \rangle \quad \text{and} \quad \beta = \langle y_1, y_2 \ldots y_n \rangle$$

is denoted by

$$\alpha \cdot \beta = \langle x_1 \ldots x_m, y_1, y_2 \ldots y_n \rangle \tag{10.2}$$

Then the range of values F denoted by (10.1) is rigorously defined by the following axioms:

1. $\langle \ \rangle$ is an F (the *empty* sequence),
2. if f is an F, and t is a T, then $f \cdot \langle t \rangle$ is an F,
3. no other values are Fs.

A file variable f is declared according to the conventions adopted in Chapter 8:

$$\textbf{var } f : F \quad \text{or} \quad \textbf{var } f : \textbf{file of } T \tag{10.3}$$

Its value is by definition always an F. For reasons to be explained in section 10.2, we will assume that with every declaration of a file variable f, an additional variable of type T is automatically introduced. This variable is to be called *buffer variable* and denoted by $f\uparrow$. It is used either to append new components to the file, or to pick its components for inspection.

Files play an essential role in every computer system. They are the appropriate structure for data to be stored on devices with mechanically moving parts for which the sequential access of components is often the only possible one, because the storage elements are led past a reading or writing device in strictly sequential order. The exact operations which a computer system can perform on a certain storage device depend on its physical design. The following devices are widely used, and the data stored on them are usually considered to be sequential files.

1. *Magnetic tapes, discs, and drums.* Reading, writing, and erasing (by repositioning and overwriting) are possible.
2. *Card readers and punches, papertape readers and punches.* In the case of readers, only sequential reading (not even repositioning) is possible. A file represented by a card deck or a papertape loaded on a reader is therefore called an *input file.* Analogously, a card deck or papertape to be generated by a punch unit is called an *output file.*
3. *Line printers.* The corresponding file whose components are supposed to be printable characters is an output file.

A file's assignment to a specific kind of device and the resulting restrictions on its processing state are specified by its so-called *disposition.* But since we are not concerned with the physical representation of data, there is no need for a notation to specify a disposition.

The concept of the file serves as an *abstraction* of data stored on any of these storage devices and allows us to formulate their common characteristics and operations in a general way. The most important file operators are described in the following sections.

10.2 GENERATING A FILE

The declaration of a file variable determines its identification, its structure and its type. Additionally, the initial number of components is 0. It is called the *length* of the file; a file with zero length is called *empty* and denoted by $\langle \rangle$. The length is increased by dynamically appending components by the standard file operator *put.* We define the operator (procedure) $put(f)$ as appending to the file f one single component. Its value is copied from the buffer variable that is implicitly introduced by the declaration of the file f (10.2). The effect of executing the statement $put(f)$ can be formally described as follows.

$$\{(f = \alpha) \wedge (f\uparrow = x)\} \quad put(f) \quad \{f = \alpha \cdot \langle x \rangle\} \tag{10.4}$$

To make efficient implementations of files on actual computers possible, it is advantageous not to make use of the value of the buffer variable $f\uparrow$ after the execution of $put(f)$. We therefore specify that the operation $put(f)$ leaves the value $f\uparrow$ undefined.

Example: Generating a file

A file of integers is to be generated that has an ith component with the value i^2 and that contains all squares of natural numbers less than n. (Note the recurrence relations

$$\left. \begin{array}{l} a_i = a_{i-1} + b_i \\ b_i = b_{i-1} + 2 \end{array} \right\} \quad \text{for } i > 1 \tag{10.5}$$

From $a_1 = b_1 = 1$, it therefore follows $a_i = i^2$.)

$$
\begin{aligned}
&\textbf{var } A, B: integer; \\
&\quad f: \textbf{file of } integer; \\
&\textbf{begin } A := 1; \quad B := 1; \\
&\quad\quad \textbf{repeat } \{A = (B + 1)^2/4\} \\
&\quad\quad\quad f\uparrow := A; \quad put(f); \\
&\quad\quad\quad B := B + 2; \quad A := A + B \\
&\quad\quad \textbf{until } A \geq n \\
&\textbf{end.}
\end{aligned}
\tag{10.6}
$$

10.3   INSPECTING A FILE

After a file has been generated, it is ready for inspection. This *inspection* proceeds strictly sequentially, starting with the first component in the file. During inspection, the file is characterized by a *position*, which divides the file into the part that has already been inspected and the part that is still to be read. For example, if a file is physically represented by magnetic tape, then this position corresponds to the tape's position relative to the tape-unit's reading head.

In *file generation*, the file position is implicitly given because the new components are appended *at the end*, but in *file inspection*, the file position must necessarily be *explicit*. A convenient explicit representation is obtained by denoting the two file parts as $\overleftarrow{f}$, the part already read, and $\overrightarrow{f}$, the part to be read. Their concatenation is always the entire file:

$$
f = \overleftarrow{f} \cdot \overrightarrow{f}
\tag{10.7}
$$

The component currently being inspected can then be designated as the first element of $\overrightarrow{f}$, where

$$
first(\langle x_1, x_2, \ldots, x_n \rangle) = x_1
$$

We now introduce the standard file operator (procedure) $reset(f)$, which causes the file f to assume a starting position for inspection. Its effect can be formally described by

$$
\{f = \alpha\} \quad reset(f) \quad \{(\overleftarrow{f} = \langle \, \rangle) \wedge (\overrightarrow{f} = \alpha) \wedge (f\uparrow = first(\overrightarrow{f}))\}
\tag{10.8}
$$

This definition implies that the buffer variable $f\uparrow$ assumes the value of the first file component—if there is one. To proceed to the next component, we introduce the standard file operator (procedure) $get(f)$. This operator moves the file position one unit to the right and assigns the value of the next component to $f\uparrow$. It can be formally defined by

$$\{(\vec{\bar{f}} = \alpha) \wedge (\vec{f} = \langle x \rangle \cdot \beta)\} \quad get(f)$$
$$\{(\vec{\bar{f}} = \alpha \cdot \langle x \rangle) \wedge (\vec{f} = \beta) \wedge (f\uparrow = first(\vec{f}))\} \tag{10.9}$$

Note that the equality

$$f\uparrow = first(\vec{f})$$

is a consequence of both the *reset* and *get* operators. However, this function is defined only if $\bar{f}$ consists of at least one component, that is, if $\vec{f}$ is not empty. It is therefore important to have a facility available to test whether $\vec{f}$ is empty. We postulate this facility in the form of the standard predicate (Boolean function) $eof(f)$, which means **end of f**ile.

$$eof(f) \quad \equiv \quad \vec{f} = \langle \rangle \tag{10.10}$$

Consequently, the operations $reset(f)$ and $get(f)$ leave $f\uparrow$ defined only if $\neg eof(f)$.

In addition to the operations *put, reset, get,* and the function *eof,* we now introduce the fourth and final file operator (procedure), *rewrite(f)*. It is used to discard the value of a file variable to permit the generation of a new file with the same name. Its effect can be formally described by

$$rewrite(f) \quad \{f = \langle \rangle\} \tag{10.11}$$

The possible sequences of operations on a file are shown in (10.12). This graph clearly exhibits the fact that, in general, the "phases" of file generation and file inspection alternate.

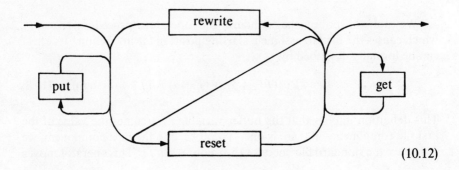

$$(10.12)$$

In many cases, the sequential structure of a file makes the repetitive statement the appropriate construct for expressing the process of file inspection. After every inspection of a file component by a statement S, the operation $get(f)$ assigns to $f\uparrow$ the value of the next component and then advances the file position. This is represented by program schema (10.13).

$$
\begin{array}{l}
\textbf{while } \neg eof(f) \textbf{ do} \\
\quad\quad \textbf{begin } S; get(f) \\
\quad\quad \textbf{end}
\end{array}
\qquad (10.13)
$$

Only if it is asserted that f is initially not empty, then may we use schema (10.14), which under this condition is equivalent to (10.13).

$$
\begin{array}{l}
\textbf{repeat } S; get(f) \\
\textbf{until } eof(f)
\end{array}
\qquad (10.14)
$$

Example: Counting of file components
The length of file f is to be determined and then assigned to the variable L. Using schema (10.13) as a basis and substituting $L := L + 1$ for S, we obtain program (10.15).

```
var L: integer;
begin L := 0;
      while ¬eof(f) do
      begin {L = number of components read}        (10.15)
          L := L + 1; get(f)
      end
end.
```

In general, it is recommended to ignore the existence of a buffer variable and to use exclusively the standard procedures *read* and *write* defined below in terms of the primitives *get* and *put*. However, sometimes it is very convenient to have the buffer variable available as a lookahead device. But in many programming languages and computing systems the buffer variable is inaccessible.

$$read(f,x) \quad \text{stands for} \quad x := f\uparrow; get(f)$$
$$write(f,x) \quad \text{stands for} \quad f\uparrow := x; put(f)$$

Program schemata (10.13) and (10.14) are then replaced by the schemata

$$
\boxed{
\begin{aligned}
&\textbf{while } \neg eof(f) \textbf{ do} \\
&\quad \textbf{begin } read(f,x); S(x) \\
&\quad \textbf{end}
\end{aligned}
} \qquad (10.15)
$$

$$
\boxed{
\begin{aligned}
&\textbf{repeat } read(f,x); S(x) \\
&\textbf{until } eof(f)
\end{aligned}
} \qquad (10.16)
$$

Since the *read* and *write* operations occur very frequently, we shall use the following abbreviations:

$$read(f, x_1, \ldots, x_n) \quad \text{stands for}$$
$$read(f, x_1); \ldots; read(f, x_n)$$
$$write(f, x_1, \ldots, x_n) \quad \text{stands for}$$
$$write(f,x_1); \ldots; write(f, x_n)$$

Example: Mean value and variance

Given a series of $n > 0$ measurements x_i represented as a file f of real numbers, compute their mean value m and their standard deviation s by applying the formulas

$$m = \frac{1}{n} \sum_i x_i, \qquad s^2 = \frac{1}{n} \sum_i (x_i - m)^2$$

Using schema (10.14), we obtain program (10.17).

```
var f: file of real;
    m,s,x: real; n: integer;
begin m:= 0; n:= 0; reset(f);
    repeat n:= n+1; read(f,x); m:= m+x
    until eof(f);                                    (10.17)
    m:= m/n; s:= 0; reset(f);
    repeat read(f,x); s:= s + sqr(x−m)
    until eof(f);
    s:= sqrt(s/n); ...
end.
```

10.4 TEXTFILES

A file whose components are printable characters is called a *textfile*. Textfiles play a fundamental role in data processing, since the input and output data of most programs are textfiles. Punched papertapes prepared on a typewriter, decks of cards prepared on keypunch machines, computed results printed on continuous paper, and data streams emanating from or directed to typewriter terminals—all of these are considered to be textfiles. A computational process using any of these media as a data carrier is considered to be a transformation, converting one textfile called *input* into another textfile called *output*.

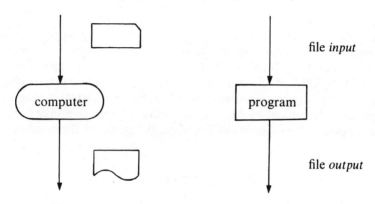

It is therefore appropriate to introduce a standard type and two *standard variables*. They are assumed to be predefined in every computer system, that is, declared implicitly as

$$\textbf{type } text = \textbf{file of } char$$
$$\textbf{var } input, output: text$$

(10.18)

The two variables are supposed to denote the two standard input and output media of any given computer system. It is therefore sensible to subject them to the following restrictions.

1. *input* can only be inspected but not repositioned or regenerated. Only the operation *get* is applicable. Its generation (cf. 10.12) occurs prior to the program's initiation.
2. *output* can only be generated but not repositioned or reread. Only the operation *put* is applicable. Its inspection (cf. 10.12) occurs after the program's termination.

Usually, a text is partitioned into lines. Hence, the question arises as to how this line structure is to be represented in terms of our file concept. There exist two essentially different methods:

1. The set of characters defined by the type *char* contains an element denoting the end of a line. This is then an instance of a so-called (non-printing) *control character*. Hence, the line structure is *implicit*.

2. Each line is considered as a sequence of characters, and the text itself is a sequence of lines. Hence, the line structure is *explicit*.

Case 1 requires no further explanations. But since many computer installations use character sets devoid of explicit control characters, case 2 merits some attention. One is tempted to regard a text as a **file of file of** *char*, but this would lead to rather tedious formulations of text processing operations. An exceptional treatment of the type *text* is therefore acceptable and desirable. It consists of the use of additional standard operators for the generation and recognition of line ends. We postulate them as follows:

$write\ln(f)$ terminate current line on file f

$read\ln(f)$ skip to the beginning of the next line

$eoln(f)$ a Boolean function; *true* after reading
the last character of a line, *false* otherwise.

In order to facilitate the reading of texts where the line structure, although present, is insignificant, we postulate the following convention: upon reading, each line end becomes manifest as a blank character, i.e. whenever $eoln(f) =$ true, then $f\uparrow = '\ '$.

For *readln* and *writeln* we accept the same notational abbreviations as for *read* and *write*. Moreover, since the two standard files are used most frequently, we assume that

1. if the file parameter is missing in a read statement, then the file *input* is assumed by default.

2. if the file parameter is missing in a write statement, then the file *output* is assumed by default.

Example: Graphic representation of a function

A real-valued function f is represented graphically with the aid of a line printer. This is possible, for instance, by printing an asterisk in positions corresponding to the coordinates $(x_0, y_0), \ldots, (x_n, y_n)$, where $x_0, \ldots, x_n$ are equidistant abscissas. We let the x-axis run along the continuous-form paper and choose a scale such that $d = x_i - x_{i-1}$ corresponds to the distance between two lines on the printed paper. The position of the asterisk at coordinate x_i is obtained by computing $y_i = f(x_i)$, multiplying y_i by a scale factor s, and rounding the product to the next integer. It represents the number of blanks that must precede the asterisk in the line. In program (10.21), the following values are used as an example.

$f(x) = exp(-x) * sin(2\pi x)$ $0 \leqq x < 4$
$d = 1/32$ (32 lines for interval $[x, x + 1]$)
$s = 50$ (50 character widths for interval $[y, y + 1]$)
$h = 65$ (distance of x-axis from edge of paper, as expressed in character position)

```
const d = 0.03125;   s = 50;   h = 65;   c = 6.28318;   lim = 128;
var x, y:real;   i, n:integer;
begin i := 0;
    repeat x := i * d;   y := exp(-x) * sin(c*x);
           n := round (s * y) + h                                    (10.21)
        repeat write(' ');   n := n - 1
        until n = 0;
        writeln('*');   i := i + 1
    until i = lim
end.
```

Textfiles are subdivided into single lines. This is a typical example of the frequently encountered subdivision of a file into *logical sections*. The individual section (here *line*) may consist of different numbers of components (here *characters*). Naturally, the subdivision of a file into logical sections has an influence on the structure of a program inspecting the file. The suitable structure of a corresponding inspection program is the *nested repetition*. The "outer" repetition processes one section at a time, and the "inner" repetition processes one file component at a time. These ideas are reflected by program schema (10.22) for the specific case where the sections are lines in a textfile.

```
while ¬eof(f) do
    begin S1;
        while ¬eoln(f) do
            begin read(f,ch); S2(ch)                    (10.22)
            end;
        S3; readln(f)
    end
```

In this schema, S2 specifies the actions to be taken for every character. S1 and S3 specify, respectively, the actions to be executed at the beginning and at the end of each line.

If it is asserted that the file consists of at least one line and each line contains at least one character, then schema (10.23) may be used instead of (10.22).

```
repeat S1;
    repeat read(f,ch); S2(ch)
    until eoln(f);                                       (10.23)
    S3; readln(f)
until eof(f)
```

Example: Insertion of printer-control characters

In connection with line printers, it is fairly customary to treat the first character in each line as a control character rather than as one to be printed. The character is interpreted as specifying the action of the paper-feed mechanism. The reason for this convention arises from the frequently used technique of temporarily storing output data in a buffer (until a printer is available, for example). The data obtained by the printer from the buffer store must contain the necessary printer control information, and its insertion in the data file in the form of an extra character at the beginning of each line has obvious advantages. Some of the control characters usually used are

    ' '   (blank) normal paper feed
    '0'   double space feed
    '1'   feed up to next page

In this example, the program will copy the file *input* to the file *output* by merely inserting the necessary one blank in each line that signals normal spacing. Program (10.24) is obtained from schema (10.22) by substituting the appropriate *write* statements in place of S1, S2, and S3.

```
        var ch: char;
        begin
            while ¬eof(input) do
            begin write(' '); {printer control}
                while ¬eoln(input) do                    (10.24)
                    begin read(ch); write(ch)
                    end;
                writeln; readln
            end
        end.
```

EXERCISES

10.1 Given two input files f and g containing the ordered sequences of integers

$$f_1, f_2, \ldots, f_m \quad \text{and} \quad g_1, g_2, \ldots, g_n$$

such that

$$f_{i+1} \geq f_i \quad \text{and} \quad g_{j+1} \geq g_j \quad \text{for all } i, j$$

design a program that merges the two files into one ordered file h such that

$$h_{k+1} \geq h_k \quad \text{for} \quad k = 1, \ldots, m + n - 1$$

10.2 Extend program (10.21) in such a way that in addition to the function $f(x)$, the x-axis is also printed.

10.3 Write a program that copies a text f onto a file g, whereby sequences of blanks are condensed into a single blank, except if standing at the beginning of a line.

10.4 Given a textfile *input* over a character set with two distinct separators (called **eop** and **eol**) which subdivide the file into paragraphs (**eop**) and the paragraphs into lines, design a program schema to inspect that file, executing the statements

$S1$ at the beginning of each paragraph
$S2$ at the beginning of each line
$S3$ for each character read inside a line
$S4$ at the end of each line
$S5$ at the end of each paragraph.

Assume that **eop** characters occur only immediately after an **eol** or another **eop** character and that the file is terminated by an **eop** character.

10.5 Given is a file f of numbers x_i. A sub-sequence $x_i \ldots x_k$ is called a *string*, if its members are ordered ($x_i \leq x_{i+1} \leq \cdots \leq x_{k-1} \leq x_k$). It is a maximal string, if also $x_{i-1} > x_i$ and $x_k > x_{k+1}$. The value $k - i + 1$ is called the length of the string.
Write a program which determines the length of the longest maximal string in the given file f.

11 THE ARRAY DATA STRUCTURE

Like a file, a variable with an array structure is a collection of *component variables of the same type*. But the following characteristics of an array create a definite distinction between the two kinds of structures.

1. Each single component of an array is explicitly denotable and directly accessible.
2. The number of its components is defined when the array variable is introduced and remains unchanged thereafter.

These characteristics make particular notational conventions necessary

(a) to denote individual array components and

(b) to define array-structured types.

Components are denoted by the name of the array variable and a so-called *index*, which uniquely designates the desired element. The fact that this index may be a computable object distinguishes the array in particular from many other data structures. These indices must therefore be of one of the available data types, which is then called the *index type* of the array. We restrict index types to those that are scalar so that a linear ordering exists among the array components, and we postulate the following notational conventions.

1. The definition of an array type includes specifications of the component type as well as the index type. There exists a unique mapping between

array components and index values. The definition of an array type takes the form

$$\textbf{type } A = \textbf{array } [T1] \textbf{ of } T2 \tag{11.1}$$

where A is the new type identifier, $T1$ denotes the index type, and $T2$ denotes the component type. Examples of array-variable declarations (with anonymous types) are

$$\textbf{var } x: \textbf{ array } [1 . . 20] \textbf{ of } real$$
$$\textbf{var } y: \textbf{ array } [color] \textbf{ of } color \tag{11.2}$$

According to these declarations, x consists of 20 components of type *real* with index values $1, 2, \ldots, 20$, and y has four components of type *color* (cf. 8) with index values *red*, *yellow*, *green*, and *blue*.

2. The component of an array variable A corresponding to the index value i is denoted by $A[i]$ or A_i. Examples (cf. 11.2) are

$$x[10] \qquad x[i + j]$$
$$y[red] \qquad y[y[yellow]] \tag{11.3}$$

Two arrays are defined as equal if and only if they are of the same type and all corresponding components are equal. Thus

$$u = v \quad \leftrightarrow \quad u_i = v_i \quad \text{for all } i \tag{11.4}$$

The requirement that every component of an array be explicitly identifiable has the natural consequence that every component be equally accessible (in a computer store). This, however, restricts considerably the selection of appropriate storage media to represent array variables. In particular, sequential storage devices such as papertapes, magnetic tapes, and magnetic discs (to a lesser degree) are all unsuitable. Storage devices where the access time is equal for all storage cells are highly desirable. The best known representatives of this class are the magnetic core store and the integrated semiconductor store, which have no mechanically moving parts. They are so-called *random-access stores*, where any cell chosen at random can be immediately accessed. But the cost of such stores is significantly higher than the cost of sequential devices, so the latter are always used to hold large volumes of data. If, however, the size of a data set is such that it still fits into the directly accessible store of a computer—the so-called *primary store* —then the array is usually the appropriate structure for this data set. In contrast to the primary store, the large volume sequential stores of a computer system are called *secondary stores*.

Example: Searching an array component

Given an array with components $A[1], \ldots, A[n]$ and a value x, set q to *false*, if there is no k such that $A[k] = x$; otherwise set q to *true* and i to k.

$$
\begin{aligned}
&\textbf{var } i: 0 \ldots n; \quad q: Boolean; \quad \{n > 0\} \\
&\quad A: \textbf{array } [1 \ldots n] \textbf{ of } T; \\
&\textbf{begin } \{\text{assignment of values to } A\} \\
&\quad i := 0; \\
&\quad \textbf{repeat } i := i + 1; \quad q := A[i] = x \\
&\qquad \{A[j] \neq x \text{ for } j = 1 \ldots i - 1\} \\
&\quad \textbf{until } q \lor (i = n) \\
&\textbf{end.}
\end{aligned}
\qquad (11.5)
$$

The termination condition of this search program is the logical union of the conditions q (the desired component is found) and $i = n$ (all components differ from x). A customary technique to simplify this composite condition and thereby to speed up the algorithm is the following;

1. The array A is extended by one component,
2. The new component is assigned the value x, and acts as a *sentinel* for the end of the search.

The resulting program is shown in (11.6).

$$
\begin{aligned}
&\overline{\textbf{var}} \ i: 0 \ldots n1; \ \{n1 := n + 1\} \\
&\quad A: \textbf{array } [1 \ldots n1] \textbf{ of } T; \\
&\textbf{begin } \{\text{assignment of values to } A[1] \ldots A[n]\} \\
&\quad i := 0; A[n1] := x; \\
&\quad \textbf{repeat } i := i + 1 \textbf{ until } A[i] = x; \\
&\qquad \{A[j] \neq x \quad \text{for } j = 1 \ldots i - 1\} \\
&\textbf{end.}
\end{aligned}
\qquad (11.6)
$$

Example: Searching a component in an ordered array

The problem here is the same as in the preceding example. However, the array components are ordered such that $A[i] < A[j]$ for all $i < j$. Although program (11.5) is also applicable in this case, we recommend a more efficient search that will take advantage of the array's ordering. An improved method is based on the following idea.

Consider the components of the array to be the nodes of a tree that has (at most) two branches at each node (and is therefore called a *binary tree*). Figure (11.7) shows a "tree" with $n = 15$ nodes.

If we select first the component in the middle with index $k = (1 + n)/2$ and compare it with x, then three possibilities exist.

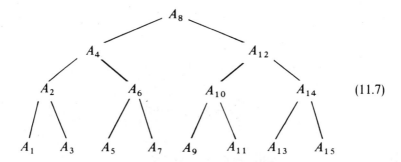

$$(11.7)$$

1. $A[k] = x$—the desired component is found.
2. $A[k] < x$—no component in the left branch may be equal to x, since all their indices j are less than k and therefore also $A[j] < A[k]$. A further search should then be restricted to the right branch.
3. $A[k] > x$—for analogous reasons, a further search here should be restricted to the left branch.

These considerations lead to program (11.8).

```
var i, j, k: integer; q: Boolean;
    A: array [1 .. n] of T;                              (11.8)
begin {assignment of values to A}
    i := 1; j := n; q := false;
    repeat k := (i + j) div 2;
        if A[k] = x then q := true else
        if A[k] < x then i := k + 1 else j := k − 1
    until q ∨ (i > j)
end.
```

The search strategy described by (11.8) is called *binary search*. Note that the number of necessary comparisons is (on the average) considerably lower than that for a linear search—namely, at most $\log_2 n$ as compared to n in (11.6). The expected mean value is even less than $\log_2 n$. Of course, binary search is applicable only if the components are ordered. (See also (11.32).)

Example: Scalar products
Given the numbers $x_1, \ldots, x_n$ and $y_1, \ldots, y_n$, compute the scalar product

$$s = \sum_{i=1}^{n} x_i * y_i \qquad (11.9)$$

The definition of this sum in terms of the recurrence relation

$$s_i = s_{i-1} + x_i * y_i, \qquad s_0 = 0 \qquad (11.10)$$

yields the program given in (11.11) as follows:

$$\textbf{var } s: real;\ i: integer;$$
$$x, y: \textbf{array } [1\ ..\ n] \textbf{ of } real;$$
$$\textbf{begin } \{\text{assignment of initial values to } x \text{ and } y\}$$
$$s := 0;\ i := 0; \hspace{3cm} (11.11)$$
$$\textbf{repeat} \left\{ s = \sum_{j=1}^{i} x[j] * y[j] \right\}$$
$$i := i + 1;\ s := s + x[i] * y[i]$$
$$\textbf{until } i = n$$
$$\textbf{end.}$$

As in example (11.6), the arrays are scanned strictly sequentially, but in contrast to (11.6), *all* components are considered at all times. The *sequence* in which they are accessed, however, is *irrelevant*—the n multiplications could even be performed concurrently.

This case occurs so frequently in the processing of array structures that a special notation is appropriate. Again, we will express it in the form of a repetitive clause similar to the **while** and **repeat** clauses. If S is the statement to be repeated, V is a scalar variable (called the *controlled* variable), and a and b are expressions of the same type as V, then the statement

$$\textbf{for } V := a \textbf{ to } b \textbf{ do } S \hspace{3cm} (11.12)$$

specifies that the two statements

$$V := x;\ S \hspace{4cm} (11.13)$$

are to be repeated, once for each value x in the interval a to b. Following the tradition of frequently used programming languages, the repetitions are executed sequentially with values x selected in ascending order from a to b. Statement (11.12) can then be regarded as equivalent to the sequence of statements (11.14)

$$\textbf{begin } V := v_1;\ S;\ V := v_2;\ S;\ \dots;\ V := v_n;\ S \textbf{ end} \hspace{1cm} (11.14)$$

where $v_1 = a$, $v_n = b$, and $v_i = succ(v_{i-1})$ for $i = 2, \dots, n$. (It follows that the successor function must be defined on the type of V, which therefore cannot be *real*.) Statement (11.14) can be represented in a closed form by program schema (11.15).

$$
\begin{aligned}
&\textbf{if } a \leq b \textbf{ then} \\
&\textbf{begin } V := a;\ S; \\
&\quad\quad \textbf{while } V < b \textbf{ do} \\
&\quad\quad\quad\quad \textbf{begin } V := succ(V);\ S \\
&\quad\quad\quad\quad \textbf{end} \\
&\textbf{end}
\end{aligned}
\hspace{2cm} (11.15)
$$

This schema reveals (among other details) that the **for** statement specifies no action if $a > b$. For $a \leq b$, the complexity of the schema is an indicator of the complexity of the corresponding verification rule, added here for the sake of completeness. Let P and $Q(V)$ be arbitrary conditions.

The preconditions are

(a) $\{(V = a) \land P\} \, S \, \{Q(a)\}$ (11.16.1)
(b) $\{Q(pred(x))\} \, S \, \{Q(x)\}$ for all $a < x \leq b$

The consequences are

(a) $\{(a \leq b) \land P\}$ **for** $V := a$ **to** b **do** S $\{Q(b)\}$
(b) $\{(a > b) \land P\}$ **for** $V := a$ **to** b **do** S $\{P\}$ (11.16.2)

The application of this inductive verification rule can be illustrated by rewriting program (11.11) in the form

$$\begin{aligned} &\textbf{begin } s := 0; \\ &\qquad \textbf{for } i := 1 \textbf{ to } n \textbf{ do } s := s + x[i] * y[i] \\ &\textbf{end} \end{aligned}$$ (11.17)

We substitute $s = 0$ for P, and $s = \sum_{j=1}^{i} x_j * y_j$ for $Q(i)$ in (11.16.1) and obtain two preconditions.

(a) $\{(i = 1) \land (s = 0)\} \, s := s + x[i] * y[i] \, \left\{ s = \sum_{j=1}^{1} x_j * y_j \right\}$ (11.18.1)

(b) $\left\{ s = \sum_{j=1}^{i-1} x_j * y_j \right\} s := s + x[i] * y[i] \left\{ s = \sum_{j=1}^{i} x_j * y_j \right\}$

Condition (b) holds for all $i = 2, \ldots, n$ and is easily verified. Then the consequence derived by the same substitution in (11.16.2) is

$$\{s = 0\} \quad \textbf{for } i := 1 \textbf{ to } n \textbf{ do } s := s + x[i] * y[i] \quad \left\{ s = \sum_{j=1}^{n} x_j * y_j \right\}$$ (11.18.2)

Obviously, condition $Q(V)$ assumes the role of the invariant in the verification rules for the **while** and **repeat** statements (7.13) and (7.14). However, an explicit identification of the controlled variable is necessary, since an assignment to this variable is implicitly specified in the **for** clause. Finally, we should note a considerable advantage offered by the **for** statement: no proof has to be given of termination. Instead, it is provided by the fact that the set of values $a, \ldots, b$ is finite.

Of course, the use of the **for** statement is not restricted to programs involving array structures. The following rule summarizes the cases in which a formulation using a **for** clause is appropriate.

If a statement is to be repeated, the use of a **for** statement is recommended when the number of necessary repetitions is known *a priori*. If their number becomes known only while the repetitions are being performed, then the **while** and **repeat** clauses are the appropriate formulations.

The following three examples will demonstrate the appropriate use of array structures and **for** statements.

Example: Finding the maximum value $x[j]$
Find the index j such that $x_j = \max(x_m, \ldots, x_n)$.

$$
\begin{aligned}
&\textbf{var } j, k: m \ldots n; \\
&\qquad x: \textbf{array } [m \ldots n] \textbf{ of } T; \\
&\textbf{begin } j := m; \\
&\qquad \textbf{for } k := m + 1 \textbf{ to } n \textbf{ do} \\
&\qquad\qquad \textbf{if } x[k] > x[j] \textbf{ then } j := k \\
&\textbf{end}
\end{aligned}
\qquad (11.19)
$$

The condition $Q(k)$ used for verification is

$$
x[j] \geqq x[i] \quad \text{for all } i = m, \ldots, k \qquad (11.20)
$$

Example: Sorting of an array
The components of an array are permuted in such a way that they appear in a decreasing order of value. To accomplish this permutation,

(a) determine the maximum element x_j according to program (11.19),
(b) exchange x_j and x_1, and
(c) repeat steps (a) and (b), considering the sets $x_2, \ldots, x_n, x_3, \ldots, x_n$, etc., until only x_n is left.

This recipe can be formulated by the statement

$$
\begin{aligned}
&\textbf{for } h := 1 \textbf{ to } n-1 \textbf{ do} \\
&\textbf{begin } \{Q(h - 1), \text{ if } h > 1\} \\
&\qquad 1: \text{Find the largest element } x_j = \max(x_h, \ldots, x_n); \\
&\qquad 2: \text{Interchange } x_h \text{ and } x_j \\
&\qquad\qquad \{Q(h)\} \\
&\textbf{end}
\end{aligned}
\qquad (11.21)
$$

Statement 1 is given in detail in (11.19), and statement 2 can be expressed as a sequence of three assignments using an auxiliary variable u.

$$
u := x[h]; \; x[h] := x[j]; \; x[j] := u \qquad (11.22)
$$

The conditions used in verifying the program are

$$P: \text{empty} \quad (\text{i.e., } true) \tag{11.23}$$
$$Q(h): x_1 \geq x_2 \geq \cdots \geq x_h \geq x_i \quad \text{for all } i > h$$

By suitable substitutions in (11.21), we finally obtain the sorting program (11.24).

```
var h, j, k:  1 .. n;
    x: array [1 .. n] of T;   u: T;
begin  ...
    for h := 1 to n − 1 do
    begin j := h;
        for k := h + 1 to n do
            if x[k] > x[j] then j := k;      (11.24)
        u := x[h]; x[h] := x[j]; x[j] := u
    end
end.
```

This program contains a **for** statement nested within another **for** statement. The statement beginning with "**if** $x[k] > x[j]$ **then** . . . " is executed

$$(n - 1) + (n - 2) + \cdots + 2 + 1 = \frac{n}{2}(n - 1) \tag{11.25}$$

times. The computational effort expended with this primitive sorting method grows roughly with the square of the number of components to be sorted. For applications with large n, the use of more sophisticated sorting methods is therefore recommended.

Components of arrays need not be scalars—they themselves may be structured. If they are again arrays, then the original array A is called *multi-dimensional*. If the components of the component arrays are scalars, then A is called a *matrix*. The declaration of a multidimensional array variable follows the pattern formulated in (11.1). For example, in the declaration

$$\textbf{var } M: \quad \textbf{array } [a .. b] \textbf{ of } \quad \textbf{array } [c .. d] \textbf{ of } \quad T \tag{11.26}$$

M is declared to consist of $b - a + 1$ components (often called matrix rows) with indices $a, \ldots, b$, each of which is an array of $d - c + 1$ components of type T with indices $c, \ldots, d$. To denote the ith component (matrix row) of M, the conventional notation

$$M[i] \quad a \leq i \leq b \tag{11.27.1}$$

is used, and its jth component of type T is denoted by

$$M[i][j] \quad a \leq i \leq b, \quad c \leq j \leq d \tag{11.27.2}$$

It is customary and convenient to use the following abbreviations, which are entirely equivalent to (11.26) and (11.27.2), respectively.

$$\textbf{var } M: \quad \textbf{array } [a \mathrel{..} b, c \mathrel{..} d] \textbf{ of } \quad T \tag{11.28}$$
$$M[i, j]$$

Example: Multiplication of matrices

Given the two real-valued matrices A ($m \times p$) and B ($p \times n$), compute the matrix product C ($m \times n$), as defined by

$$C_{ij} = \sum_{k=1}^{p} A_{ik} * B_{kj} \tag{11.29}$$

for $i = 1, \ldots, m$ and $j = 1, \ldots, n$.

The formulation of program (11.30) follows from (11.29) in a straightforward manner.

```
var i:1..m;  j:1..n;  k:1..p;  s:real;
    A: array [1 .. m, 1 .. p] of real;
    B: array [1 .. p, 1 .. n] of real;
    C: array [1 .. m, 1 .. n] of real;
    begin {assignment of initial values to A and B}
        for i := 1 to m do
            for j := 1 to n do                              (11.30)
                begin  s := 0;
                    for k := 1 to p do s := s + A[i, k] * B[k, j];
                    C[i, j] := s
                end
    end.
```

This program is an example of a multiple nesting of repetitive statements. Since such programs invariably involve relatively large amounts of computation, a closer analysis of the ensuing effort is appropriate. It is evident that the repetition on i is executed m times, the one on j $m * n$ times, and the one on k $m * n * p$ times. Assuming that m, n, and p are large ($\gg 1$), the effort expended on the statement

$$s := s + A[i, k] * B[k, j]$$

dominates completely. From this, we learn the simple but important lesson that the "innermost" repeated statement should be formulated with the greatest care to minimize computation and maximize efficiency. The effort spent on a matrix multiplication grows with the *third* power of n, assuming that $m = n = p$ [cf. Exercise (11.8)].

EXERCISES

11.1 Let the matrix A be given as

$$A = \begin{pmatrix} 2 & 1 & 3 \\ 3 & 3 & 1 \\ 1 & 2 & 1 \end{pmatrix}$$

(a) Execute the statement

$$\textbf{for } i := 1 \textbf{ to } 3 \textbf{ do} \qquad\qquad (11.31)$$
$$\textbf{for } j := 1 \textbf{ to } 3 \textbf{ do } C[i,j] := A[A[i,j], A[j,i]]$$

Which is the resulting value C?

(b) Is the order in which the indices i and j are chosen relevant?

(c) In (11.31), replace the variable C by A. What is the resulting value of A?

(d) Repeat part (c) by taking the following reversed sequence of index pairs for i and j.

$$(3,3), (3,2) \ldots (1,2), (1,1)$$

Compare the resulting A with the one obtained in (c).

11.2 Verify the following version of the binary search program

$$i := m; j := n;$$
$$\textbf{repeat } k := (i + j) \textbf{ div } 2;$$
$$\qquad \textbf{if } A[k] \leq x \textbf{ then } i := k + 1; \qquad\qquad (11.32)$$
$$\qquad \textbf{if } A[k] \geq x \textbf{ then } j := k - 1$$
$$\textbf{until } i > j$$

Compare the number of necessary comparisons with those in program (11.8), noting that the termination condition is simpler in (11.32).

11.3 A complex-valued matrix Z is represented by a pair $\langle X, Y \rangle$ of real-valued matrices such that $Z = X + iY$. Design a program to compute the product of two complex valued matrices $\langle A, B \rangle$ and $\langle C, D \rangle$; that is,

$$X + iY = (A + iB) * (C + iD) \qquad\qquad (11.33)$$

Hint:

$$(A + iB) * (C + iD) = (AC - BD) + i(AD + BC) \qquad\qquad (11.34)$$

Compute the three matrices

$$R = A * D, \qquad S = B * C, \qquad T = (A + B) * (C - D)$$

and then

$$X = T + R - S \quad \text{and} \quad Y = R + S$$

Determine the number of required additions and multiplications (as a function of the matrix size n) and compare them with those obtained when using (11.33) directly.

11.4 A polynomial

$$P_n(x) = a_0 x^n + a_1 x^{n-1} + \cdots + a_{n-1} x + a_n \qquad (11.35)$$

is represented by the array of coefficients a. Design a program computing $P_n(x)$ for a given x. *Hint*: Use factorization according to *Horner*; that is,

$$P_n(x) = (\cdots (a_0 x + a_1) * x + \cdots + a_{n-1}) * x + a_n \qquad (11.36)$$

11.5 Design a program that finds the largest and the smallest value in an array of n numbers

$$\textbf{var } A\colon \textbf{array } [1 \ldots n] \textbf{ of } integer$$

Hint: It is possible to do this using less than $(3/2)n$ comparisons.

11.6 Given an array variable

$$\textbf{var } M\colon \textbf{array } [1 \ldots n, 1 \ldots n] \textbf{ of } integer$$

construct a program that assigns the natural numbers $1, 2, \ldots, n^2$ to the components of M such that it forms a *magic square*; that is,

$$\sum_{k=1}^{n} M[i, k] = \sum_{k=1}^{n} M[k, i] = C \qquad i = 1, \ldots, n$$

and

$$\sum_{k=1}^{n} M[k, k] = \sum_{k=1}^{n} M[k, n-k+1] = C$$

where $C = (n/2)(n^2 + 1)$. Assume n to be odd. *Hint*: Assign the numbers $1, \ldots, n^2$ sequentially to components of M, starting with 1 at $M[i, j] = M[(n+1)/2, n]$, then increasing i and j by 1 (modulo n) each time for $n - 1$ steps, and decreasing j by 1 and leaving i unchanged in every nth step.

11.7 Given the problem to compute the first $n + 1$ terms in the series representing the sine function [cf. (9.29)] for arguments x such that $0 \le x \le \pi/4$, the following program was designed. (s is supposedly the result.)

```
    var i: integer; h, s: real;
        t: array [0 .. n] of real;                          (11.37)
    begin t[0] := x; h := sqr(x); s := x;
        for i := 1 to n do
            t[i] := − t[i−1] * h/(2*i * (2*i + 1));
        for i := 1 to n do s := s + t[i]
    end.
```

Is the program correct? What should be criticized?

11.8 Given are two real-valued matrices X and Y with $2n$ rows and columns. Construct a program to compute the matrix product $Z = X * Y$, using the following relation (due to Winograd) to compute the necessary scalar products [cf. (11.29)].

$$\sum_{k=1}^{2n} x_k * y_k = \sum_{k=1}^{n} (x_{2k} + y_{2k-1}) * (x_{2k-1} + y_{2k})$$

(11.38)

$$- \underbrace{\sum_{k=1}^{n} x_{2k} * x_{2k-1}}_{\bar{x}} - \underbrace{\sum_{k=1}^{n} y_{2k} * y_{2k-1}}_{\bar{y}}$$

Hint: The problem requires the computation of $4n^2$ scalar products of the form

$$\sum_{k=1}^{2n} x_{ik} * y_{kj}$$

Using (11.38), only $2n$ values $\bar{x}$ and $\bar{y}$ are needed.

The usual method of matrix multiplication (11.30) requires $8n^3$ additions and multiplications. Determine the number of operations required by your program as a function of n.

12 SUBROUTINES, PROCEDURES, AND FUNCTIONS

12.1 CONCEPT AND TERMINOLOGY

Frequently, a certain sequence of statements has to be repeated at various places within a program. To save the programmer the time and effort needed to recopy these statements, most programming languages offer a *subroutine* (subprogram) facility. This device makes it possible to assign a freely chosen name to the sequence of statements and then to use that name as an abbreviation wherever that sequence of statements occurs. Following ALGOL terminology, we will call such named sequences of statements *procedures*. If the procedures also represent a resulting value and may therefore be used within expressions, they are called *functions*. The definition of the abbreviation is called *procedure declaration* or *function declaration*. Its use in the program is called a *procedure statement* or *procedure call*. A function specified within an expression is called a *function designator* or *function call*.

The particular notation used for procedure declarations and procedure statements can be found in the syntax diagrams in Appendix A and in the examples in this chapter.

Example: Procedure declaration and statement
The sequence of statements

$$t := r \bmod q; \quad r := q; \quad q := t \tag{12.1}$$

can be abbreviated by using the procedure declaration in (12.2).

$$\begin{aligned} &\textbf{procedure } P; \\ &\textbf{begin } t := r \bmod q; r := q; q := t\textbf{end} \end{aligned} \tag{12.2}$$

The sequence, wherever it occurs, can then be replaced by the procedure statement

$$P \tag{12.3}$$

A procedure declaration consists of two parts: the *procedure heading* and the *procedure body*. The heading (first line, 12.2) contains the identifier of the procedure. The body (second line in 12.2) consists of the statement(s) to be abbreviated.

We would not make an issue out of such simple notational conventions, unless some important, basic concepts were involved. Actually, the procedure is one of the few fundamental tools in the art of programming whose mastery has a decisive influence on the style and the quality of a programmer's work. The procedure serves as a device to abbreviate the text and, more significantly, as a means to partition and to structure a program into logically coherent, closed components. Partitioning is essential in understanding a program, particularly if it is so complex that the text assumes a length that is impossible to survey at a glance. Structuring into subroutines is indispensable both in documenting and in verifying the program. Therefore, it is often desirable to formulate a sequence of statements as a procedure —even when it occurs only once and the motivation of shortening the text is therefore absent. Additional information about variables (those being inspected or those altered by the procedure) or about conditions that must be satisfied by the arguments, may be provided conveniently in the heading of the procedure.

Two other basic programming concepts emphasize the usefulness of the procedure, particularly its role in program structuring. Frequently, certain variables or objects (often called *auxiliary variables*) used within a given sequence of statements have no significance whatsoever outside those statements. The perspicuity of a program is definitely enhanced by clearly exhibiting the scope of significance of such objects. The procedure appears to be the natural textual unit by which to delineate the *scope of validity* of so-called *local objects*.

Equally frequent is the case where a certain sequence of statements appears in various places of the program in not exactly identical but highly similar form. Particularly important is the situation where the difference between the individual occurrences of the statements can be eliminated by systematic substitutions of identifiers or expressions. In this case, the statements to be abbreviated can be abstracted into a *procedure schema*. The entities still to be substituted for the individual occurrences are called *procedure parameters*.

12.2 LOCALITY

If an object—a constant, a variable, a procedure, a function, or a type— is significant only within a certain part of the program, it is called *local*. In such cases, it is appropriate to give that section of the program a name (i.e., to formulate it as a procedure). The local objects are then declared in the heading of the procedure. Since procedures themselves may be defined locally, procedure declarations may be nested.

Example: Procedure declaration with local variable declaration

$$\textbf{procedure } P;$$
$$\textbf{var } t: integer; \quad (12.4)$$
$$\textbf{begin } t := r \textbf{ mod } q; r := q; q := t \textbf{ end}$$

Inside the procedure body, two kinds of objects are used; local objects (t) and nonlocal objects. The latter are declared in the *environment* of the procedure declaration. If they are defined in the main program, they are called *global*, and if they are defined in the language (i.e., in the context in which the program is "embedded"), they are called *standard*. The scope of validity of local objects is the entire text of the procedure. This implies that after termination of the process described by a procedure, the storage space used for local variables becomes available again and can be used for other variables. Obviously, in a later activation (call) of the same procedure, the values of its local variables are again undefined, just as they were in the first activation.

In the identification of local objects, it is essential that the names can be freely chosen without regard to the environment. But a situation may then arise in which the identifier (say, x) that was chosen for a local variable in procedure P is identical with that of an object in the environment of P. Of course, this situation makes sense only if the nonlocal x is of no significance to P. We will therefore adopt the basic convention that in a case of a conflict of names, x within P will denote the local variable, and x outside of P will denote the nonlocal object.

Example: Procedure with apparent conflict of identifiers (d)

$$\textbf{var } a, b, d, e: integer; \quad \{\text{global variables}\}$$
$$\textbf{procedure } Multiply; \quad \{\text{global procedure}\}$$
$$\textbf{var } c, d: integer; \quad \{\text{local variables}\}$$
$$\textbf{begin } \{e := a * b, \text{cf. (7.18)}\} \quad (12.5)$$
$$c := a; d := b; e := 0;$$
$$\textbf{while } d \neq 0 \textbf{ do}$$
$$\textbf{begin if } odd(d) \textbf{ then } e := e + c;$$
$$c := 2 * c; d := d \textbf{ div } 2$$
$$\textbf{end}$$
$$\textbf{end};$$
$$\textbf{begin } \{\text{main program}\} a := 5; \quad b := 7; \quad d := 10; \quad Multiply$$
$$\{a = 5, b = 7, d = 10, e = 35\}$$
$$\textbf{end.}$$

It is convenient to consider the main program as a procedure without a name. Its environment is the operating system of the computer, where all standard objects are predefined. This view also explains why identifiers may be chosen without respect to the postulated standard names. So long as a standard object is not used in the program, either accidental or intentional use of its identifier as a name for a local object has no adverse effect whatsoever.

12.3 PROCEDURE PARAMETERS

If a particular sequence of operations is applied to *different* operands in different parts of a program, the sequence is formulated as a *procedure*, and the operands become *parameters*. The identifiers introduced in the procedure heading to denote the operands are called *formal parameters*. They are used only within the procedure body and are local to it. The objects to be substituted for the formal parameters are called *actual parameters*. They are specified in each procedure statement or function designator. The *type* of the actual parameter is determined by the type of the formal parameter, as specified in the procedure heading. Besides specifying the type of the parameter, it also is necessary to indicate the *kind* of substitution desired, since either the current value or the identity of the actual variable or expression may be substituted. It is customary to distinguish three kinds of parameter substitutions.

1. The actual parameter is evaluated, and the resulting value is substituted for the corresponding formal parameter. This is called *value substitution*. It is the most commonly encountered situation.
2. The actual parameter is a variable; possible indices are evaluated; and the variable thereby identified is then substituted for its formal correspondence. This is called *variable (reference) substitution*. It is used if the parameter represents a result of the procedure.
3. The actual parameter is substituted literally, and no evaluation occurs. This is called *substitution-by-name*. It occurs rarely in practical applications.

Example:
The effects of the three kinds of parameter substitutions are demonstrated by program (12.6). We investigate the consequences of the procedure statement $P(a[i])$.

$$
\begin{aligned}
&\textbf{var } i: integer; \\
&\quad a: \textbf{array } [1 \mathinner{.\,.} 2] \textbf{ of } integer; \\
&\textbf{procedure } P(x: integer); \\
&\quad \textbf{begin } i := i + 1; \quad x := x + 2 \\
&\quad \textbf{end}; \\
&\textbf{begin } \{\text{Main program}\} \\
&\quad a[1] := 10; \quad a[2] := 20; \quad i := 1; \\
&\quad P(a[i]) \\
&\textbf{end.}
\end{aligned}
\tag{12.6}
$$

Case 1:   *Value Substitution*
            x is a variable with initial value 10.
            Final value of $a = (10, 20)$.

Case 2:   *Variable Substitution*
            $x \equiv a[1]$
            Statement $x := x + 2$ now means $a[1] := a[1] + 2$.
            Final value of $a = (12, 20)$.

Case 3:   *Substitution-by-Name*
            $x \equiv a[i]$
            Statement $x := x + 2$ now means $a[i] := a[i] + 2$.
            Final value of $a = (10, 22)$.

To distinguish the different kinds of substitution, we postulate the following notational rules.

1. *Value substitution* is the most frequent form of substitution, and is taken by default, unless an explicit specifier is supplied.
2. *Variable substitution* is indicated by the symbol **var** in front of the formal parameter(s).
3. We refrain from introducing a notation for *substitution-by-name*, because equivalent situations are treated in Section 12.4.

According to these conventions, we can rewrite program (12.5) in the form of a procedure with three parameters as shown in (12.7).

Example: *Procedure with parameters*

```
var a, b, c, d, e, f: integer;
procedure Multiply(x, y: integer; var z: integer);
    {x, y, z are the formal parameters}
begin z := 0;
    while x ≠ 0 do                                        (12.7)
    begin if odd(x) then z := z + y;
            y := 2 * y;   x := x div 2
    end
end;
begin {Main program}
    a := 5;   b := 7;   d := 11;   e := 13;
    Multiply(a, b, c);   Multiply(d − b, e − a, f)
    {a = 5, b = 7, c = 35, d = 11, e = 13, f = 32}
end.
```

Program (12.7) shows that in the case of value substitution, the formal parameter denotes a local variable that has initially been assigned the result of the evaluation of the corresponding actual parameter. After this initial assignment, however, there no longer exists any "connection" between the actual and the formal objects. This allows us to formulate two general rules governing the choice of substitutions.

1. If a parameter is an argument rather than a result of a procedure (function), then a *value substitution* is (usually) appropriate.
2. If a parameter acts as result of a procedure, then a *variable substitution* is necessary.

Certain pitfalls are inherent in the variable-substitution method. They arise because the *same* variable can be made accessible under more than one identification. This is particularly dangerous when dealing with structured variables such as arrays. In such cases, it is imperative that the programmer adhere strictly to the following important rule of programming discipline: Every *variable parameter must be disjoint from all other parameters*; that is, no parameter should denote the whole or a component of any other parameter. The potential dangers in violating this rule are shown in the following example of a simple matrix-multiplication procedure.

Example: Pitfalls of variable parameters

```
type matrix = array [1 .. 2, 1 .. 2] of integer;
procedure mult (var x, y, z: matrix);                    (12.8)
begin z[1, 1] := x[1, 1] * y[1, 1] + x[1, 2] * y[2, 1];
      z[1, 2] := x[1, 1] * y[1, 2] + x[1, 2] * y[2, 2];
      z[2, 1] := x[2, 1] * y[1, 1] + x[2, 2] * y[2, 1];
      z[2, 2] := x[2, 1] * y[1, 2] + x[2, 2] * y[2, 2];
end
```

Given the matrices

$$A = \begin{pmatrix} 2 & 1 \\ -1 & 3 \end{pmatrix} \quad \text{and} \quad B = \begin{pmatrix} 3 & -1 \\ 1 & 2 \end{pmatrix}$$

we can investigate the effects of the following procedure statements.

1. $mult(A, B, C)$ yields $C = \begin{pmatrix} 7 & 0 \\ 0 & 7 \end{pmatrix}$.

2. $mult(A, B, A)$ yields $A = \begin{pmatrix} 7 & -5 \\ 0 & 6 \end{pmatrix}$.

3. $mult(A, B, B)$ yields $B = \begin{pmatrix} 7 & 0 \\ -4 & 6 \end{pmatrix}$.

Note that the correct results in statement 1 can be obtained in all three cases, if x and y are specified as value parameters [see also Exercise 11.1].

12.4 PARAMETRIC PROCEDURES AND FUNCTIONS

A procedure or function F is used as a parameter of a procedure or function G, if F is to be computed during the execution of G, and if F represents different procedures or functions in different calls of G. Well-known examples are algorithms to compute an integral G of a function F.

Example: Simpson integration
To approximate the integral

$$s = \int_a^b f(x)\,dx \tag{12.9}$$

we compute the sum of a finite number of sample values f_i.

$$s_k = \frac{h}{3}(f_0 + 4f_1 + 2f_2 + 4f_3 + 2f_4 + \cdots + 4f_{n-3} + 2f_{n-2} + 4f_{n-1} + f_n) \tag{12.10}$$

where $f_i = f(a + i * h)$, $h = (b - a)/n$, and $n = 2^k$. The number of sample points is $n + 1$, and h is the distance between any two adjacent sample points. The integral value s is then approximated by the sequence $s_1, s_2, s_3, \ldots$, which converges if the function is sufficiently well behaved (smooth) and if an exact arithmetic is assumed.

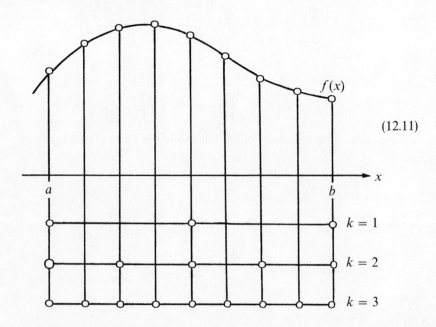

$$\tag{12.11}$$

In each step, the number of sample points is doubled. Of course, a well-designed program will avoid evaluating the function 2^k times in each kth step; instead, it will reuse the f_i values computed in earlier steps. The sum s_k is therefore represented by the three terms

$$s_k = s_k^{(1)} + s_k^{(2)} + s_k^{(4)} \qquad (12.12)$$

which denote the sums of the sample points with weights 1, 2, and 4, respectively. They can be defined in terms of the recurrence relations in (12.13), for $k > 1$, and the initial values in (12.14).

$$s_k^{(1)} = \tfrac{1}{2} s_{k-1}^{(1)}$$

$$s_k^{(2)} = \tfrac{1}{2} s_{k-1}^{(2)} + \tfrac{1}{4} s_{k-1}^{(4)} \qquad (12.13)$$

$$s_k^{(4)} = \frac{4h}{3}(f(a + h) + f(a + 3h) + \cdots + f(a + (n - 1)h)$$

$$s_1^{(1)} = \frac{h}{3}(f(a) + f(b))$$

$$s_1^{(2)} = 0 \qquad (12.14)$$

$$s_1^{(4)} = \frac{4h}{3} f\left(\frac{a + b}{2}\right)$$

When appropriately substituted in program schema (9.23), these relations yield the integration program (12.15), which is formulated as a function with f as parameter.

```
function Simpson (a, b: real; function f: real): real;
    var i, n: integer;
        s, ss, s1, s2, s4, h: real;
```

{ $f(x)$ is a real-valued function with a single, real-valued parameter. The function must be well-defined in the interval $a \le x \le b$}

```
begin n := 2; h := (b - a) * 0.5;
    s1 := h * (f(a) + f(b)); s2 := 0;
    s4 := 4 * h * f(a + h); s := s1 + s2 + s4;        (12.15)
    repeat ss := s; n := 2 * n; h := h/2;
        s1 := 0.5 * s1; s2 := 0.5 * s2 + 0.25 * s4;
        s4 := 0; i := 1;
        repeat s4 := s4 + f(a + i * h); i := i + 2
        until i > n;
        s4 := 4 * h * s4; s := s1 + s2 + s4
    until abs(s-ss) < ε;
    Simpson := s/3
end
```

The function *Simpson* can now be used as an operand in any real expression. For instance, the statement

$$u := Simpson\ (0,\ \pi/2,\ sin) \tag{12.16}$$

denotes the assignment

$$u = \int_0^{\pi/2} \sin(x)\,\mathrm{d}x$$

However, only a function identifier may occur as an actual third parameter. In most programming languages, the use of an expression is not allowed. (The notable exception is ALGOL 60 with the so-called name-parameter facility.) For instance, to compute

$$u = \int_0^{\pi/2} \frac{\mathrm{d}x}{(a^2 \cos^2 x + b^2 \sin^2 x)^{\frac{1}{4}}} \tag{12.17}$$

using the *Simpson* function, another function, *F*, must be explicitly declared. Thus

$$\textbf{function } F(x: real): real; \tag{12.18}$$
$$\textbf{begin } F := 1/sqrt(sqr(a * cos(x)) + sqr(b * sin(x)))\ \textbf{end}$$

Only then is it possible to express (12.17) by the statement

$$u := Simpson(0,\ \pi/2,\ F) \tag{12.19}$$

EXERCISES

12.1 Formulate programs (7.18), (7.22), (9.17), (9.28), (10.21), (11.24), and (11.30) as procedures or functions with suitably chosen parameters.

12.2 Consider the function declaration

$$\textbf{function } f(x, y: real): real;$$
$$\textbf{begin if } x \geq y \textbf{ then } f := (x + y)/2 \textbf{ else} \tag{12.20}$$
$$f := f(f(x + 2, y - 1), f(x + 1, y - 2))$$
$$\textbf{end}$$

What is the value of $f(1, 10)$?
How can $f(a, b)$ be represented and computed in a simpler way?

12.3 Execute the following three programs and determine the values of the actual parameters of the *write* statements.

(a)   **var** a, b, c: *integer*;
       procedure $P(x, y$: *integer*; **var** z: *integer*);
       begin $z := x + y + z$; *write*(x, y, z)
       end;   (12.21)
     begin $a := 5; b := 8; c := 3$;
       $P(a, b, c)$; $P(7, a+b+c, a)$; $P(a * b, a$ **div** $b, c)$
     end.

(b)   **var** i, j, k: *integer*;
       procedure $P($**var** i: *integer*);
       begin $i := i + 1$; *write*(i, j, k)
       end $\{P\}$;
       procedure $Q(h$: *integer*; **var** j: *integer*);   (12.22)
          var i: *integer*;
          procedure R;
          begin $i := i + 1$
          end $\{R\}$;
       begin $i := j$;
          if $h = 0$ **then** $P(j)$ **else if** $h = 1$ **then** $P(i)$ **else** R;
          write(i, j, k)
       end $\{Q\}$;
     begin $i := 0; j := 1; k := 2$; $Q(0, k)$; $Q(1, i)$; $Q(2, j)$
     end.

(c)   **procedure** $P($**procedure** R; b: Boolean);
          var x: *integer*;
          procedure Q;
          begin $x := x + 1$
          end $\{Q\}$;   (12.23)
       begin $x := 0$; **if** b **then** $P(Q, false)$ **else** R;
       write(x)
     end $\{P\}$;
     begin $P(P, true)$
     end.

12.4 According to *Gauss*, the elliptic integral (see 12.17)

$$I = \frac{2}{\pi} \int_0^{\pi/2} \frac{dx}{(a^2 \cos^2 x + b^2 \sin^2 x)^{\frac{1}{2}}}$$

is equal to the limit of any of the two convergent sequences

$$s_0, s_1, s_2, \ldots \quad \text{or} \quad t_0, t_1, t_2, \ldots$$

as defined by the recurrence relations for $i > 0$. Thus

$$s_i = (s_{i-1} + t_{i-1})/2$$

$$t_i = \sqrt{s_{i-1} * t_{i-1}}$$

and $s_0 = a$, $t_0 = b$. The calculation of the two sequences is called the arithmetic-geometric mean method. Formulate a suitable function declaration.

12.5 The *Romberg* integration method approximates the integral

$$\int_a^b f(x)\, dx$$

by the sequence

$$t_{0,0}, t_{1,0}, t_{2,0}, \ldots$$

which is convergent for sufficiently well-behaved (smooth) functions f. The terms are defined by the recurrence relation

$$t_{m,k} = \frac{1}{4^m - 1}(4^m * t_{m-1,k+1} - t_{m-1,k})$$

for $m > 0$, and by the initial functions

$$t_{0,k} = \frac{b - a}{n}\ (\tfrac{1}{2}f_0 + f_1 + \ldots + f_{n-1} + \tfrac{1}{2}f_n)$$

where $n = 2^k$ and $f_i = f(a + i * (b - a)/n)$. Formulate a function declaration with parameters a, b, and f and approximate the integral (according to Romberg) to a specified relative accuracy ε. *Hint*: The program must evaluate the function f only once at each sample point. In each step, the number of sample points is doubled. Use an array variable T such that after the kth step

$$T[i] = t_{k-i,i} \qquad i = 0, \ldots, k$$

In case of bad convergence, the iteration should be terminated after, at most, p steps; that is, $k = 0, \ldots, p$.

12.6 Let a "zero" of a real-valued function $f(x)$ be defined as the value x_0 such that

$$(f(x_0 - \varepsilon) < 0) = (f(x_0 + \varepsilon) > 0)$$

if ε is chosen arbitrarily small. Design a function program with parameters a, b, and f that determines a zero of $f(x)$ in the interval $a \leq x \leq b$ if the relation

$$(f(a) < 0) = (f(b) > 0)$$

is guaranteed to hold. *Hint*: Use the method of repeated halving of the interval containing the zero. Note the similarity of this method, called *bisection*, to binary searching (see 11.32). How many evaluations of f are necessary if a, b, and ε are given?

13 TRANSFORMATIONS OF NUMBER REPRESENTATIONS

The abstract notion of a number is independent of its possible representations. Operations on numbers can be precisely defined by sets of general axioms. If these operations are to be performed on specific numbers, however, then a particular representation must be chosen so that the result will be recognizable.

The reason for defining operations on numbers by generally valid algorithms without reference to a specific representation lies in the desire to enable the processor charged with the execution of arithmetic operations to choose the representation most suitable to its capabilities. Modern digital computers, given this freedom of choice, use representations based on the binary alphabet. Their notation, however, is unsuitable for humans, who have been trained from early childhood to use the decimal system. Input and output devices of computers are therefore equipped with character sets containing decimal digits (which, of course, are internally encoded in terms of bits). Upon receiving and emitting numeric data, computers are then instructed to transform the externally used representation into its internally used form and vice versa. The characteristics of the common decimal-number representation are

(a) the positional notation of digits weighted by powers of a so-called base B, and
(b) the choice of 10 as the number of distinct digits and as the base.

The generalization of the problem of representation conversion algorithms to systems with arbitrary base $B (>1)$ does not introduce any additional complications. The treatment of conversion algorithms will, however, be restricted to *positional number systems*. Thus the choice $B = 10$ represents the decimal system as a specific instance. Positional number systems have the common property that the sequence $\delta_n = d_1 \ldots d_n$ of n digits denotes the number

$$\tilde{\delta}_n = \sum_{i=1}^{n} \tilde{d}_i * B^{n-i} = (\cdots (\tilde{d}_1 * B + \tilde{d}_2) * B + \cdots + \tilde{d}_{n-1}) * B + \tilde{d}_n \qquad (13.1)$$

where $\tilde{d}_i$ is the numerical value represented by the character (digit) d_i and B is the base of the number system. Every number $x(0 \leq x < B^n)$ is uniquely represented, if there are exactly B distinct digits with values $0, 1, \ldots, B\text{-}1$ available. If the first i digits representing a number are denoted by $\delta_i = d_1 \ldots d_i$, then recurrence relation (13.2) immediately follows from (13.1) with $\tilde{\delta}_0 = 0$.

$$\tilde{\delta}_i = \tilde{\delta}_{i-1} * B + \tilde{d}_i \qquad 0 \leq \tilde{d}_i < B \qquad (13.2)$$

From (13.2), it also follows that

$$\tilde{\delta}_{i-1} = \tilde{\delta}_i \ \mathbf{div} \ B \quad \text{and} \quad \tilde{d}_i = \tilde{\delta}_i \ \mathbf{mod} \ B \quad [\text{cf. also } 7.23] \qquad (13.3)$$

In subsequent programs, the representation function $\tilde{d}$ will be written as $num(d)$ with a domain restricted to single characters (digits). At the same time, its inverse will be denoted by $rep(x)$ such that

$$rep(num(d)) = d \quad \text{and} \quad num(rep(x)) = x \qquad (13.4)$$

These functions are dependent on the specific character set used. For the ASCII character set, for example, they can be expressed in terms of the primitive standard transfer functions chr and ord:

$$rep(x) \equiv chr(x + ord('0')) \quad \text{and} \quad num(d) \equiv ord(d) - ord('0') \qquad (13.5)$$

The inverse algorithm to compute a sequence of digits $d_1 \ldots d_n = \delta_n$. The purpose of the programs here is to extend these primitive transfer functions to numbers larger than B and to entire sequences of digits, respectively.

13.1 INPUT AND OUTPUT OF NON-NEGATIVE INTEGERS IN POSITIONAL FORM

A program to compute the number that is represented by a sequence of digits on a textfile D is obtained by applying recurrence relation (13.2) to program schema (9.2) and using a **repeat** statement instead of a **while** statement. The program is formulated as a procedure in (13.6), which assumes that on entry the buffer variable $D\uparrow$ represents the first digit d_1. It further assumes that the digits are followed by a character that is not a digit and it will proceed to read D until that character has been assigned to $D\uparrow$.

This scheme is most appropriate when an input file has to be read, where sequences of digits are embedded within a general text (in a program, for example).

$$\textbf{procedure } read(\textbf{var } x: integer);$$
$$\textbf{begin } x := 0; \qquad\qquad (13.6)$$
$$\textbf{repeat } x := B * x + num(D\uparrow); get(D)$$
$$\textbf{until } \neg\, digit(D\uparrow)$$
$$\textbf{end}$$

The Boolean function $digit(d)$ depends, like $num(d)$, on the underlying character set *char*. For the ASCII character set, for instance, it is expressed as

$$digit(d) \equiv ('0' \le d) \wedge (d \le '9') \qquad (13.7)$$

The inverse algorithm to compute a sequence of digits $d_1 \ldots d_n = \delta_n$ representing a number $\tilde{\delta}_n$ in the positional number system with base B is obtained by applying equations (13.3) to program schema (9.2), and by again using a **repeat** instead of a **while** statement. Given a number $\tilde{\delta}_i$, its last digit in that representation is obtained by dividing it by B and by applying the primitive transfer function $rep(x)$ to the resulting remainder. The remaining digits are obtained by applying the same algorithm to the quotient.

If the digits $d_1, \ldots, d_n$ are to be appended to an output file D, then the fact that the algorithm generates them in reverse order (the last digit is generated first) is inconvenient. It requires a buffer store, most conveniently represented by an array variable d. This yields program (13.8), which is again formulated as a procedure.

$$\textbf{procedure } write(x: integer);$$
$$\textbf{var } u: integer; i: 0 .. n; \qquad\qquad (13.8)$$
$$d: \textbf{array } [1 .. n] \textbf{ of } char;$$
$$\textbf{begin } \{0 \le x < B^n\}\ u := x; i := n;$$
$$\textbf{repeat } d[i] := rep(u \textbf{ mod } B); u := u \textbf{ div } B;$$
$$i := i - 1$$
$$\textbf{until } i = 0;$$
$$\textbf{repeat } \{\text{output digits in reverse order}\}$$
$$i := i + 1; D\uparrow := d[i]; put(D)$$
$$\textbf{until } i = n$$
$$\textbf{end}$$

This program can be easily improved in two respects.

1. To suppress leading zeroes, the termination condition of the first repetition is changed from $i = 0$ to $u = 0$. Note that one digit is still issued, even if $x = 0$.

2. By introducing an auxiliary variable v, the two statements involving the (usually expensive) **div** and **mod** operations are replaced by

$$v := u \text{ div } B; \; d[i] := rep(u - B * v); \; u := v$$

13.2 OUTPUT OF FRACTIONS IN POSITIONAL FORM

In positional number systems, real numbers are represented by an integer part and a fraction, separated by a (decimal) point. Since the problem of converting a natural number into a sequence of digits was discussed in Section 13.1, we can restrict any further discussion to the development of an algorithm to convert pure fractions x $(0 \leq x < 1)$. Again, a number system with base B is assumed.

Given is a sequence of digits $\delta = d_1 \ldots d_n$ denoting a fraction. With the point to its left, the value $\tilde{\delta}$ is defined as

$$\tilde{\delta} = \sum_{i=1}^{n} d_i * B^{-i} = \frac{1}{B}\left(\tilde{d}_1 + \frac{1}{B}\left(\tilde{d}_2 + \cdots + \frac{1}{B}\tilde{d}_n\right) \cdots\right) \tag{13.9}$$

where $\tilde{d}_i = num(d_i)$ and $0 \leq \tilde{d}_i < B$ for all i. Denoting the sequences $d_i \ldots d_n$ by δ_i, recurrence relations (13.10) follow immediately from (13.9).

$$\tilde{\delta}_i = \frac{1}{B}(\tilde{d}_i + \tilde{\delta}_{i+1}) \qquad 0 \leq \tilde{\delta}_i < 1$$

and

$$\tilde{d}_i = trunc(B * \tilde{\delta}_i)$$
$$\tilde{\delta}_{i+1} = B * \tilde{\delta}_i - \tilde{d}_i \tag{13.10}$$

The algorithm obtained by substituting (13.10) in program schema (9.2) is shown in the form of a procedure in (13.11). The variable u assumes the sequence of values $\tilde{\delta}_1, \tilde{\delta}_2, \ldots$, and the termination condition is not (as could be expected) $u = 0$, since this would imply an exact representation of the fraction $x = \tilde{\delta}$, which may not exist. The algorithm is therefore terminated when a given number n of digits has been generated. In each step, the fraction is multiplied by the base B. The integer part of the product, applied to the primitive function $rep(x)$, yields the next digit, and the same algorithm applied to the fraction part of the product yields the remaining digits. Fortunately, this procedure generates the digits in the desired order; hence intermediate storing in a buffer can be avoided. The digits are again to be appended to an output textfile D.

$$
\begin{aligned}
&\textbf{procedure } \textit{write } (x : \text{real}); \{0 \leq x < 1\}\ \text{'} \\
&\quad \textbf{var } i: 0 \ldots n;\ u: \textit{real};\ v: \textit{integer};\ \{n > 0\} \\
&\textbf{begin } u := x;\ D\!\uparrow := \text{'}.\text{'};\ put(D);\ i := 0; \\
&\quad \textbf{repeat } u := B * u;\ v := \textit{trunc}(u); \\
&\quad\quad\quad D\!\uparrow := rep(v);\ put(D); \\
&\quad\quad\quad u := u - v;\ i := i + 1 \\
&\quad \textbf{until } i = n \\
&\textbf{end}
\end{aligned}
\tag{13.11}
$$

13.3 TRANSFORMATION OF FLOATING-POINT REPRESENTATIONS

As we mentioned in Section 8.4, computers frequently use the so-called floating-point form to represent real numbers. A number x is then represented by a pair of scaled integers $\langle m, e \rangle_B$ such that

$$
x = m * B^e \qquad \frac{1}{B} \leq m < 1
\tag{13.12}
$$

where B is called the base of the floating-point system. Examples that should make the term "floating-point" self-explanatory are

$$\langle 0.34567, 2 \rangle = 34.567$$

$$\langle 0.34567, 4 \rangle = 3456.7 \qquad B = 10
\tag{13.13}$$

$$\langle 0.34567, -2 \rangle = 0.0034567$$

It is advantageous to choose a small power of 2 (say, 2^k) as the base for representations within computers. Increasing or decreasing the exponent e by 1 then corresponds to multiplying or dividing the coefficient m by 2^k, which can be performed in this case by simply shifting m by k bit positions to the left or right, respectively. Since, however, it is customary to use $B = 10$ in representations external to computers, an exponent base transformation (in addition to the radix transformation) becomes necessary when inputting or outputting floating-point numbers.

The most straightforward method of transforming the representation $\langle m_1, e_1 \rangle_{B_1}$ into the representation $\langle m_2, e_2 \rangle_{B_2}$ is to multiply m_1 by $B_1^{e_1}$ and thereafter to normalize, that is, to repeat dividing (or multiplying), the product by B_2, until $1/B_2 \leq m < 1$ is satisfied. The number of divisions is then the resulting exponent e_2. But the intermediate products may become very large and exceed the capacity of a storage cell, since m is represented as a scaled integer. We therefore impose the restriction that the conditions

$$\frac{1}{B} \leq m < B \qquad B = B_1 * B_2 \qquad (13.14)$$

be satisfied at any time—that is, after every intermediate step of computation. In a transformation from a system with base B_1 to a system with base B_2, multiplications of m by B_1 and divisions by B_2 must therefore necessarily alternate. The resulting program for $B_2 > B_1$ is shown in (13.15). For evident reasons, a distinction is made between the cases $e_1 \geq 0$ and $e_1 < 0$. Note the importance of the specified invariant in the verification of the program.

```
procedure convert(var m: real; var e1, e2: integer);
begin e2 := 0;
    if e1 ≥ 0 then                                              (13.15)
        while e1 ≠ 0 do
        begin {x = m * B₁^e1 * B₂^e2, 1/B₂ ≤ m < 1}
            m := B₁ * m; e1 := e1 − 1;
            if m ≥ 1 then begin m := m/B₂; e2 := e2 + 1 end
        end
    else repeat {x = m * B₁^e1 * B₂^e2, 1/B₂ ≤ m < 1}
            m := m/B₁; e1 := e1 + 1;
            if m < 1/B₂ then begin m := B₂ * m; e₂ := e2 − 1 end
        until e1 = 0
end
```

Considering that in real computers numbers can be represented only by a finite number of digits, this algorithm has the disadvantage of being both inefficient for large exponents e, and inaccurate, due to the accumulation of rounding and truncation errors in the long sequence of arithmetic operations. One possibility of improving this algorithm lies in storing a table of multipliers B_1^b in the form of pairs of scaled integers $\langle u, v \rangle_k$ such that

$$u_k * B_2^{v_k} = B_1^k \qquad \frac{1}{B_2} \leq u_k < 1 \qquad (13.16)$$

and then computing

$$m := m * u_{e1}, \qquad e2 := v_{e1} \qquad (13.17)$$

followed possibly by postnormalization. However, the size of such a table may be intolerably large, if the range of the exponent e_1 is large. An acceptable compromise, requiring slightly more computations but based on a much smaller table, consists of tabulating coefficient exponent pairs only for

$$u_k * B_2^{v_k} = B_1^{(2^k)} \qquad \frac{1}{B_2} \leq u_k < 1 \qquad (13.18)$$

and then decomposing the exponent $e1$ into a series of powers of 2, analogous to the multiplication algorithm (7.18). The resulting m and $e2$ are obtained as products and sums of the corresponding table entries u_k and v_k, respectively [cf. Exercise 13.3].

EXERCISES

13.1 Formulate two procedures that
  (a) read a decimal number represented by a sign, an integer part, a decimal point, and a fraction from the textfile *input* and assign its value to the real parametric variable v [cf. (13.6)], and
  (b) write a decimal representation of a real parameter x onto the file *output* [cf. (13.8) and (13.11)]. Assume that $|x| \leq max$ and that the integer and fraction parts of x are represented by m and n digits, respectively. Leading zeroes should be replaced by blanks.

13.2 Write two procedures to transform floating-point representations
  (a) with base 2 to base 10, and
  (b) with base 10 to base 2.
  Both should be similar to program (13.15).

13.3 Design a procedure to transform a floating-point representation with base 2 into a representation with base 10, using a table of n coefficient exponent pairs according to (13.18). Assume that
$$x = m * 2^{e1} \qquad 0 \leq el < 2^n$$
for a given n (say, 10).

13.4 Construct a program that generates exact decimal representations of the fractions $1/n$ for $n = 2, 3, \ldots, 50$ as described below and write the resulting digit sequences onto the file *output*.
  (a) Each digit sequence should terminate as soon as the first period of the decimal fraction is completed.
  (b) A blank should be inserted immediately preceding the first digit of the period.
  (c) No real-valued variables should be used in this program.

  Printing the textfile will result in the following picture:
$$.5\ 0$$
$$.3$$
$$.25\ 0$$
$$.2\ 0$$
$$.1\ 6$$
$$.142857$$
$$\ldots\ldots$$
$$.02\ 0$$

  Hint: First develop a program ignoring condition (b).

13.5 Design a procedure to write onto the textfile *output* the value of the integer parameter x as a Roman numeral. Assume $x > 0$. ('I' $= 1$, 'V' $= 5$, 'D' $= 10$, 'L' $= 50$, 'C' $= 100$, 'D' $= 500$, 'M' $= 1000$.)

14

PROCESSING OF TEXT USING ARRAY AND FILE STRUCTURES

In this chapter we will investigate some problems whose only common characteristic is the fact that the computed data are structures of printable characters, that is, texts. These examples, typical of many other related problems, can also serve as exercises in the application of concepts and techniques that have already been introduced.

14.1 ADJUSTING THE LENGTH OF LINES IN A TEXTFILE

If a textfile f consists of sub-sequences of characters that are delineated by either blanks or end-of-line characters, let each such sub-sequence, which does not itself contain either blanks or **eol** characters, be called a *word*. The number of characters in a word is then called the wordlength w. The number of characters in a line is called the linelength L.

A program will be developed that reads a file f and then generates a file g consisting of the same unsplit words in the same sequence but having lines that are at most *Lmax* characters long.* The total number of characters in the two files will be the same. All words in f will be of length $w \leq wmax < Lmax$ for given *wmax* and *Lmax*. Assume that file f consists of at least one word and therefore at least one line, terminated by an **eol** character.

File g is obtained by copying f and replacing certain blanks by **eol** characters and vice versa. Since individual words cannot be split, and since files can be generated only sequentially, a word can be appended to g only when it is known whether it is to be preceded by a blank or by an **eol** character.

* P. Naur, "Programming by Action Clusters," *BIT* 9 (1969), 250–258.

This, however, can be decided only after the length of the word is known. It therefore follows that copying the word is possible only through intermediate buffering. As a buffer, an array variable with *wmax* components is the appropriate choice (assuming that *wmax* is moderately small).

Since file *f* consists of a sequence of words and separator characters, the appropriate structure of the program is a repetitive statement. In each repetition, a word W and its *succeeding* separator S are read from file *f*, and the same word and its *preceding* separator are then output to file *g*, as shown in figure (14.1).

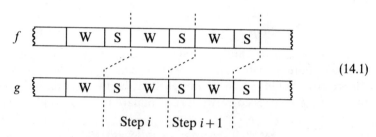

(14.1)

A case in which several separators follow a word (i.e., multiple space or several blank lines) is handled by assuming that words may be empty and that an empty word lies between every two immediately adjacent separators. In this way, the strictly alternating character of the word/separator sequence is (hypothetically) maintained.

The repeated statement is obtained from program schema (10.13). As auxiliary tools, we first introduce two informally defined procedures.

1. *Readword* reads a word into the buffer variable Z. After execution of *readword*, *ch* represents the separator following the word just read and stored in Z. The integer variable *w* is assigned the wordlength.

2. *Writeword* appends the word of length *w* stored in Z to file *g*.

Since the length of the currently generated line evidently plays an important role, a variable L is introduced to represent the currently attained length. The statement to be executed in each step can then be formulated as

$$
\begin{aligned}
&\textbf{begin } readword; \\
&\quad \textbf{if } L + w < Lmax \textbf{ then} \\
&\quad\quad \textbf{begin } write(' \ '); L := L + 1 \\
&\quad\quad \textbf{end else} \\
&\quad\quad \textbf{begin } writeln; L := 0 \\
&\quad\quad \textbf{end}; \\
&\quad writeword \\
&\textbf{end}
\end{aligned}
\qquad (14.2)
$$

Before specifying the two procedures in greater detail, we draw our attention to another problem, namely, the situation at the start and the end of· the process. Figure (14.3) indicates that it is apparently necessary to provide some statements at the beginning and at the end of the program that do not fit the pattern of statement (14.2).

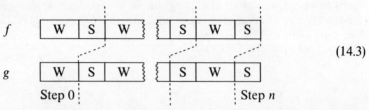

$$(14.3)$$

In the initial step, one more character is read than is written, and in the final step, one more is written than is read. The final program is shown in (14.4). The reader should convince himself that the two auxiliary procedures do process empty words correctly. (The standard files *input* and *output* are used instead of *f* and *g*).

```
var w: 0 .. wmax; {wordlength}
    L: 0 .. Lmax; {linelength}
    ch: char; {last character read}
    Z: array [1 .. wmax] of char; {buffer}
procedure readword;
begin w := 0;
    while do
        begin w := w + 1; Z[w] := ch; read(ch)
        end
end;
procedure writeword;
    var i: 1 .. wmax;                                    (14.4)
begin for i := 1 to w do write(Z[i]); L := L + w
end;
begin L := 0; read(ch); readword; writeword;
    while ¬eof(input) do
    begin read(ch); readword;
        if L + w < Lmax then
            begin write(' '); L := L + 1
            end else
            begin writeIn; L := 0
            end;
        writeword
    end;
    writeIn
end.
```

From this example, we learn two lessons.

1. If a sequence of data patterns is transformed into a sequence of corresponding patterns, then the general step of transforming a single pattern should be formulated first. The resulting statement is then subjected to a **repeat** or **while** clause characterizing the repetition and the termination conditions. The boundary situations are finally expressed by additional statements preceding and succeeding the repetition.
2. To express logical units of operations, the so-called *action clusters*, suitable procedures are introduced whose detailed specification may be deferred until later. The definition of a concrete data structure for variables that are used only inside these procedures can also be delayed—namely, until specific reasons are available to justify the choice of one structure over the others.

14.2   EDITING A LINE OF TEXT

Consider the following problem. Given are a line of text z represented by the character sequence

$$z = z_1 z_2 \ldots z_n \qquad n > 0 \qquad (14.5)$$

a sequence x (usually within z), which is to be replaced,

$$x = x_1 x_2 \ldots x_k \qquad k > 0$$

and a sequence y, which is to be substituted for x

$$y = y_1 y_2 \ldots y_m \qquad m \geq 0$$

The value *true* is to be assigned to a Boolean variable q, if and only if x is contained in z and a substitution of y is possible. To define uniquely the desired action in the case where x occurs more than once within z, we introduce a *line position p*. At any time, the text z is to be searched sequentially from left to right, starting at position p. If x is not found between p and the end, the search will continue at the beginning of z up to p. The line is thereby considered to wrap around, and the search is called circular. For example, if $x = AB$ and $y = UVW$, then z—before and after the substitution process—would be

Before:	EFABGH	After:	EFUVWGH
	EFABCDABCD		EFABCDUVWCD
	EFABCDABCD		EFUVWCDABCD

This kind of text substitution is often found in text editing systems used remotely through terminals, where programs and data are stored permanently within the computer system as textfiles.

The problem may be broken up into two relatively independent parts:

(a) the search for text x to be replaced so that $z = \alpha x \beta$, and
(b) the substitution of x by y so that $z = \alpha y \beta$.

Part 1:   An index i is determined such that

$$x_j = z_{i+j-1} \quad \text{for } j = 1, \ldots, k \tag{14.6}$$

A program that assigns to q the value "x was found and i is the desired index" is shown in (14.7).

$$
\begin{aligned}
&i := p; \\
&\textbf{repeat } \{Q(i)\} \\
&\quad q := x = (z_i \ldots z_{i+k-1}); \\
&\quad i := i + 1; \textbf{ if } i > n \textbf{ then } i := 1 \\
&\textbf{until } q \vee (i = p)
\end{aligned} \tag{14.7}
$$

The invariant assertion $Q(i)$ is

$$(x_1 \ldots x_k) \neq (z_j \ldots z_{j+k-1})$$

$$\text{for all } j = \begin{cases} p, \ldots, i-1 & \text{if } i \geqq p \\ p, \ldots, n \quad \text{and} \quad 1, \ldots, i-1 & \text{if } i < p \end{cases}$$

We now further decompose the comparison of two sequences of characters into a sequence of comparisons of single characters.

$$
\begin{aligned}
&j := 1; \\
&\textbf{repeat } \{P(j)\} \\
&\quad q := (x[j] = z[i+j-1]); \quad j := j + 1 \\
&\textbf{until } \neg q \vee (j > k)
\end{aligned} \tag{14.8}
$$

The invariant assertion $P(j)$ is equal to

$$Q(i) \wedge (x_h = z_{i+h-1}) \quad \text{for all } h = 1, \ldots, j-1$$

But this program is incomplete because it does not properly handle the following situation. Assume that

$$x_h = z_{i+h-1} \quad \text{for } h = 1, \ldots, h' \tag{14.9}$$

$$i + h' - 1 = n \qquad h' < k$$

In this case, the next characters to be compared are x_{h+1} and z_{n+1}. However, z_{n+1} is not defined. This fact also reveals that the formulation of the problem is incomplete, since it contains no specification of the behavior of the program for this situation. Should the algorithm terminate with $q = false$, or should the text $x_1 \ldots x_k$ also be considered to wrap around? If z is considered to be a line, the latter does not ordinarily make sense. Assuming that the problem statement intentionally leaves the choice open, we opt for the former interpretation.

$$
\begin{aligned}
&j := 1; \\
&\textbf{repeat if } i + j > n \textbf{ then } q := false \textbf{ else} \qquad\qquad (14.10)\\
&\qquad\quad q := x[j] = z[i+j-1]; j := j + 1 \\
&\textbf{until } \neg q \lor (j > k)
\end{aligned}
$$

Often, a specific technique is applied to simplify this program: explicit testing for the end-of-the-line is made superfluous by appending a *sentinel* character that occurs neither within z nor within x (e.g., $z_{n+1} = \textbf{eol}$). Under these circumstances, the simpler program (14.8) may be used. [cf. also (11.6)].

Part 2.: The characters $z_i \ldots z_{i+k-1}$ are now replaced by $y_1 \ldots y_m$. This operation could again be split into two steps: (a) shortening $z = \alpha x \beta$ into $z' = \alpha \beta$ (by shifting β to the left by k positions) and (b) inserting y to obtain $z'' = \alpha y \beta$ (by first shifting β to the right by m positions). Since this process can be simplified to shifting β only once, however, a distinction has to be made between the following cases.

1. $m < k$—the new sequence is shorter than the old one; β is shifted to the left by $k-m$ positions.
2. $m > k$—the new sequence is longer than the old one; β is shifted to the right by $m-k$ positions.
3. $m = k$—the new and old sequences have the same length, no shifting is necessary.

The entire program, consisting of the search and the substitution steps, is shown in (14.11).

```
procedure Substitute;
    var i, j: 1..n+1;  q: Boolean;  d: integer;
begin {step 1: find x in line z}
    i := p;
    repeat j := 1;
        repeat q: = (x[j] = z[i+j-1]);  j := j + 1
        until ¬q ∨ (j > k);
        i := i + 1; if i > n then i := 1
    until q ∨ (i = p);
```

if q **then**
begin {step 2: substitute y for x}
    $d := m - k;\ p := i;$
    if $d < 0$ **then**
    begin $j := p + k;$
        while $j \leq n$ **do**
        begin $z[j + d] := z[j];\ j := j + 1$
        end
    end else
    if $d > 0$ **then**
    begin $j := n;$
        while $j \geq p + k$ **do**
        begin $z[j + d] := z[j];\ j := j - 1$
        end
    end;
    $n := n + d;\ j := 1;$
    while $j \leq m$ **do**
    begin $z[p] := y[j];\ p := p + 1;\ j := j + 1$
    end
  end
end

$$(14.11)$$

14.3 RECOGNITION OF REGULAR PATTERNS OF SYMBOLS

The recognition of patterns of text is a frequently encountered problem, common to all programs designed to interpret or to process text in certain ways. In general, a pattern is defined by a set of composition rules. The overall complexity of a program designed to recognize patterns evidently depends on the complexity or generality of the formation rules. Sets of such rules are commonly called a *syntax*, and the task of recognizing patterns constructed according to the rules is called *syntactic analysis*.

We will introduce a class of simple rules, that is, a schema of rules. Every rule designed according to the schema defines a set of so-called *sentences*, which can be recognized by a simple analysis algorithm. The syntax rules generated by the schema display a certain regularity of structure and are therefore called *regular expressions*. Analogously, the set of sentences that can be generated according to a regular expression is called a *regular language*.

Our specific task is to provide some general construction rules indicating how to construct systematically a recognition program that corresponds to a given syntactic rule. We introduce the following notational conventions.

1. Small Latin letters denote symbols of the basic vocabulary V. All sentences are sequences of symbols from V.
2. Capital letters denote regular expressions or the set of sentences (the regular language) defined by the regular expression.
3. Greek letters denote sequences of symbols over the vocabulary V. ε denotes the empty sequence.
4. The set of sequences of symbols obtained by concatenating or juxtaposing a sentence of A and a sentence of B is called the product of A and B.

$$AB = \{\alpha\beta ; \alpha \in A \text{ and } \beta \in B\} \tag{14.12}$$

5. The sum or union of A and B is denoted by

$$A \mid B = \{\gamma ; \gamma \in A \text{ or } \gamma \in B\} \tag{14.13}$$

6. The set of sequences obtained by concatenating sentences of A an arbitrary number of times is denoted by A^*.

$$A^* = \{\varepsilon|A|AA|AAA\ldots\} \tag{14.14}$$

The formation rules for regular expressions are the following.

1. Every basic symbol $a \in V$ is a regular expression.
2. Every product of two regular expressions is a regular expression.
3. Every union of two regular expressions is a regular expression.
4. If A is a regular expression, then A^* is a regular expression.
5. Only expressions obtained by rules 1–4 are regular.

The following are examples of regular expressions over the vocabulary $V = \{a\,b\,c\,d\}$. Parentheses are used as bracketing symbols in the usual manner.

1. a
2. $(ab|bc)(d|a)$ (14.15)
3. ab^*c
4. $a((b|c)a)^*$

The sets of sentences defined by these expressions are the following.

1. a
2. $abd \quad aba \quad bcd \quad bca$ (14.16)
3. $ac \quad abc \quad abbc \quad abbbc\ldots$
4. $a \quad aba \quad aca \quad ababa \quad abaca \quad acaba \quad acaca\ldots$

Our task may now be reformulated: given a regular expression A defining a set of sentences over the vocabulary V and given any sequence α of symbols over V, construct an algorithm $\mathscr{P}(A)$ that determines whether α is a sentence of A (i.e., $\alpha \in A$).

The possibility of representing regular expressions in terms of a graph is both obvious and attractive. Each of the elementary formation rules of regular expressions translates immediately into a graphic pattern as follows:

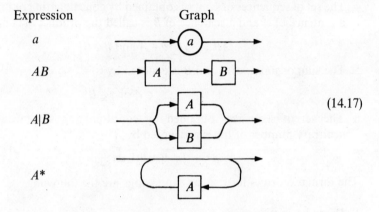

(14.17)

For example, the application of these correspondences to expression 4 in (14.15) results in the following graph.

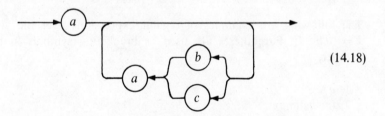

(14.18)

The graphs immediately suggest a form of the algorithm that can recognize sentences, if the traversal of a circled basic symbol in the graph is interpreted as the recognition of that symbol in the sequence α to be analyzed, and if the traversal of the entire graph is interpreted as the acceptance of the entire sentence.

Let us now assume that the sequence α to be analyzed is represented by the textfile *input*, implying that the basic symbols are characters and that only sequential access is possible. Our aim is to construct an algorithm to analyse sentences *without backing up* and without the aid of intermediate buffering (so-called *look ahead*) as a substitute for back-up. Briefly, the algorithm should be such that every decision (represented by a fork of paths in the graph) can be taken by inspecting the next single character only.

We thus describe a scheme by which an analysis algorithm can be methodically constructed from a given expression. However, the construction rules apply only if the expression is *deterministic*, that is, if it contains no constituents of the forms

$$A|B \quad \text{and} \quad A*B \tag{14.19}$$

such that A and B have common initial symbols. Any initial symbol s of a sentence of A is called an initial symbol of A. Examples of regular expressions and their deterministic equivalents (assuming that A and B have no common initial symbols) are

$$aA|aB = a(A|B)$$
$$(aA)*aB = a(Aa)*B \tag{14.20}$$

and

$$(aA)*a|(aB)*a = a((Aa)*|(Ba)*)$$

The construction rules are given below, where $\mathcal{P}(X)$ denotes the program schema corresponding to the regular expression X. We assume that there is a variable ch to which the next symbol to be inspected is always assigned and that there exists a procedure $test(x)$ verifying the equality $ch = x$.

Construction rules

1. $\mathcal{P}(a)$ = $test(a)$; $read(ch)$
2. $\mathcal{P}(AB)$ = $\mathcal{P}(A)$; $\mathcal{P}(B)$ (14.21)
3. $\mathcal{P}(aA|B)$ =   **if** $ch = a$ **then**
                begin $read(ch)$; $\mathcal{P}(A)$ **end**
            else $\mathcal{P}(B)$
4. $\mathcal{P}((aA)*)$ =   **while** $ch = a$ **do**
                begin $read(ch)$; $\mathcal{P}(A)$ **end**

To obtain a complete program corresponding to an expression A followed by a sentence terminator (e.g. a period), the schema $\mathcal{P}(A)$ is embedded in the following "frame."

         var ch: $char$;
         begin $read(ch)$; $\mathcal{P}(A)$; $\{ch = ' \cdot '\}$ (14.22)
         end.

Examples of analysis programs generated from given deterministic regular expressions according to these construction rules follow.

1. $\mathscr{P}(ab^*c) =$

    test(*a*); *read*(*ch*);

    while *ch* = *b* **do** *read*(*ch*);   (14.23)

    test(*c*); *read*(*ch*)

2. $\mathscr{P}(a(b(c|d))^*e) =$

    test(*a*); *read*(*ch*);

    while *ch* = *b* **do**

        begin *read*(*ch*);

            if *ch* = *c* **then** *read*(*ch*) **else**

            begin *test*(*d*); *read*(*ch*)

            end

        end;

    test(*e*); *read*(*ch*)

3. $P((ab^*c)^*d) =$

        while *ch* = *a* **do**

        begin *read*(*ch*);

            while *ch* = *b* **do** *read*(*ch*);

            test(*c*); *read*(*ch*)

        end;

        test(*d*); *read*(*ch*)

The purpose of the procedure *test*(*x*) was specified as the verification of the equality *ch* = *x*. If the relation is not satisfied, the sequence of inspected characters is not a sentence of the language specified by the underlying regular expression, and the analysis process may as well be terminated (aborted). For example, this action may be specified by a **goto** statement (jump) of the form

$$\textbf{goto } L \qquad\qquad (14.24)$$

where *L* is a label marking the destination of the jump. Any statement in a program may be marked by prefixing the statement with the label and a colon. The **goto** statement should be reserved for situations that are "unusual" or "uncommon"—that is, where the natural structure of an algorithm has to be broken (e.g., the detection of a formation of input data that violates the given specifications). A good rule is to avoid the use of jumps to express regular iterations and conditional execution of statements, since with the introduction of explicit jumps, the structure of a computation is no longer reflected by the textual structure of its program. Moreover, this lack of correspondence between textual and computational structure is extremely detrimental to the clarity of programs and makes the task of verification much more difficult.

Algorithms for the analysis of textual patterns are the basis of programs that process structured texts (e.g., compilers, which translate or interpret programs). They are essentially programs constructed by inserting additional statements within the program structures performing the syntactic analysis. These other statements compute a translated text from the inspected text. With their addition, the mere analysis process (generating a Boolean answer) becomes a translation process, where encountering an ill-structured input text cannot, in general, be satisfactorily met by a simple abortion with a jump to the program end. Nevertheless, an algorithm serving as a framework for superimposed translation procedures will significantly enhance the reliability and trustworthiness of a translator, if it is constructed methodically and systematically according to a given set of rules.

EXERCISES

14.1 Determine whether the following programs correctly solve the problem in Section 14.1.

(a) **var** i, L, w: *integer*; *ch*: *char*;

$\quad\quad Z$: **array** $[1 .. wmax]$ **of** *char*;　　　　　　　　　　　　　　　　(14.25)

$\quad$ **begin** $L := 0$;

$\quad\quad$ **repeat** $w := 0$; *read* (ch);

$\quad\quad\quad$ **while** $ch \neq$ ' ' **do**

$\quad\quad\quad\quad$ **begin** $w := w + 1$; $Z[w] := ch$; *read(ch)*

$\quad\quad\quad\quad$ **end**;

$\quad\quad\quad$ **if** $w > 0$ **then**

$\quad\quad\quad\quad$ **begin if** $L + w < Lmax$ **then**

$\quad\quad\quad\quad\quad$ **begin** *write* (' '); $L := L + 1$

$\quad\quad\quad\quad\quad$ **end else**

$\quad\quad\quad\quad\quad$ **begin** *writeIn*; $L := 0$

$\quad\quad\quad\quad\quad$ **end**;

$\quad\quad\quad\quad$ **for** $i := 1$ **to** w **do** *write*$(z[i])$; $\ L := L + w$

$\quad\quad\quad$ **end**

$\quad\quad$ **until** *eof (input)*

$\quad$ **end.**

(b) **var** i, L, w: *integer*; *ch*: *char*;

$\quad\quad Z$: **array** $[1 .. wmax]$ **of** *char*;

$\quad$ **begin** $L := Lmax$;

$\quad\quad$ **repeat if** $ch =$ ' ' **then** *read(ch)* **else**

$\quad\quad\quad$ **begin** $w := 0$;

$\quad\quad\quad\quad$ **repeat** $w := w + 1$; $Z[w] := ch$; *read(ch)*

$\quad\quad\quad\quad$ **until** $ch =$ ' '

```
                    if L + w < Lmax then
                        begin write(' '); L := L + 1
                        end else
                        begin writeIn; L := 0
                        end;
                    for i := 1 to w do write(Z[i]);  L := L + w
                end
            until eof (input);
            writeIn
    end.
```

14.2 In a printed line of length L, certain characters are marked. The marks are represented by a specific character (say, '*') printed below each such character. The positions (indices) of the marked characters are given in the form of an array

$$p_1, p_2, \cdots, p_n \qquad n \geq 0, \qquad 1 \leq p_i \leq L$$

with the relations

$$p_i \leq p_j \quad \text{for all } i < j$$

Example: $p = (3, 6, 9, 19, 22), n = 5$
   Line of text: Thes broplem is peenuds.
   Line of marks: * * *   * *

Investigate the following proposals. Which ones are correct? Indicate the conditions under which the incorrect ones fail.

(a) $k := 1$;
```
    for i := 1 to L do
    begin if i = p[k] then
            begin write('*'); k := k + 1
            end
            else write(' ')
    end
```

(b) $k := 1; p[n + 1] := 0$;
```
    for i := 1 to L do
    begin if i = p[k] then
            begin write('*');
                repeat k := k + 1 until i ≠ p[k]
            end
            else write(' ')
    end
```

(c) $i := 1$;
```
    for k := 1 to n do
    begin repeat write(' '); i := i + 1
            until i = p[k];
        write('*'); i := i + 1
    end
```

(d) $i := 1; k := 1;$
```
repeat
    while i < p[k] do
        begin write(' '); i := i + 1
        end;
    if i = p[k] then
        begin write('*'); i := i + 1
        end;
    k := k + 1
until k > n
```

(e) $i := 1; k := 1;$
```
while k ≤ n do
begin while i < p[k] do
        begin write(' '); i := i + 1
        end;
        while p[k] = i do k := k + 1;
        write('*')
end
```

14.3 Design a program that counts the number of occurrences of each character in the file f. Represent the result by a variable N, declared as

$$\textbf{var } N: \textbf{array } [char] \textbf{ of } integer$$

such that $N[c]$ denotes the number of occurrences of the character c in f. Furthermore, a variable D should indicate the number of counts not equal to zero.

14.4 Given are two arrays A and B of so-called words, that is, sequences of letters. Specifically, for $i = 1, \ldots, M$,

$$A_{i,1} \ldots A_{i,m_i} \quad \text{and} \quad B_{i,1} \ldots B_{i,n_i} \quad m_i, n_i < N$$

are letters, and

$$A_{i,m_i+1} \ldots A_{i,N} \quad \text{and} \quad B_{i,n_i+1} \ldots B_{i,N}$$

are blanks.

Also given is a file *input* consisting of words (sequences of letters) separated by blanks and/or end-of-line characters.

Design a program that reads the file *input* and generates a file *output* by replacing all words equal to some A_i by the corresponding word B_i. *Hint:* The buffer to be used must consist of at most N characters. Use the procedure *Transmitword*, which compares the word in the buffer Z with A and appends to *output* either B_i (if $Z = A_i$) or Z (if there is no $A_i = Z$). Be careful when adopting the following unverified procedure. $(Z = Z_1 \ldots Z_k)$

```
procedure Transmitword;
    var i: 0..M;  j: 0..N;  f: Boolean;
    begin i := 0; {Z[k + 1] = ' ', 0 < k < N}
        repeat i := i + 1; j := 0;
```

$$\textbf{repeat } j := j + 1; f := Z[j] \neq A[i,j]$$
$$\textbf{until } f \vee (j = k)$$
$$\textbf{until } \neg f \vee (i = M);$$
$$\textbf{if } f \textbf{ then } Emit(Z) \textbf{ else } Emit(B[i])$$
$$\textbf{end}$$

14.5 Given an array S of so-called key words, let $S_{i,1}, \cdots, S_{i,n_i}$ be letters and $1 \leq n_i < N$. As in Exercise 14.4, a file *input* is given consisting of words (sequences of letters) separated by blanks and/or end-of-line characters. Every line contains at most L characters.

Design a program that generates a file output consisting of the same lines as input but rotated so that the beginning of a key word lies at a fixed position k. If there is no key word in a line, then this line does not appear in the output file; if a line contains n key words, then this line appears n times, each time being differently rotated. A buffer variable with at most L characters should be used.

14.6 Develop a program according to the construction rules (14.21) and (14.22) for the analysis of arithmetic expressions. The vocabulary is

$$V = \{\lambda + - * / \cdot\}$$

where λ stands for any letter. The structure of the input is given by the regular expression

$$\lambda((*|/)\lambda)^*((+|-)\lambda((*|/)\lambda)^*)^*.$$

15 STEPWISE PROGRAM DEVELOPMENT

Our examples in the preceding chapters have clearly shown that programming—in the sense of designing and formulating algorithms—is in general a complicated process, requiring the mastery of numerous details and specific techniques. It is also obvious that only in exceptional cases will there be a single good solution. Usually, so many solutions exist that the choice of an optimal program requires a thorough analysis not only of the available algorithms and computers but also of the way in which the program will most frequently be used. If programming were a strictly deterministic process obeying a fixed set of rules, then it would have been automated long ago.

As in other engineering disciplines, the construction of a product—in this case, an algorithm—consists of a sequence of deliberations, investigations, and design decisions. In the early stages, attention is directed mainly toward the global problems, and the first draft of a solution may pay little attention to details. As the design process progresses, the problem is split up into subproblems, and gradually more consideration is given to the details of problem specification and to the characteristics of the available tools. In programming, the abstract nature of the products designed is particularly intriguing. In contrast to other areas of engineering, the products can be designed (and tested) without material expenditures, and they are free from the physical side effects of aging and materials of inferior quality. Consequently, programmers should be particularly keen to develop many versions of algorithms and to carefully compare and analyze them before making a final choice.

Perhaps the most general programming strategy involves partitioning a process into individual actions and the corresponding program into individual statements. In each such step of decomposition, one has to be sure that

(a) the solutions of the partial problems imply the solution of the total problem,

125

(b) the chosen sequence of component actions is meaningful, and
(c) the selected decomposition yields statements that, in some sense, are closer to the language in which the program will ultimately be formulated.

It is precisely this last requirement that makes progress in a straight line from the original problem to the ultimate program impossible. Each decomposition step is followed by the task of formulating partial programs, during which the choice of decomposition may turn out to be unfortunate in one sense or another simply because the subroutines may not be conveniently expressed in terms of the underlying tool. One or more of the previously taken steps must then be reconsidered.

If one views the stepwise decomposition of the problem and the simultaneous development and refinement of the program as a gradual progression to greater and greater depth, it can be characterized as the *top-down* approach to problem solving. Inversely, it is also possible to postulate an approach whereby the programmer first considers his computer and/or programming language and then groups certain instruction sequences together into primitive procedures or "action clusters," which will typically occur in the underlying problem. The primitive procedures are then used within the next hierarchy of procedures. This approach—from the depths of primitive, atomic machine instructions to the problem at the surface—is called the *bottom-up* method. In practice, the development of a program can never be performed either in a strictly top-down or a pure bottom-up direction. In general, however, the top-down approach is dominant, when a new algorithm is conceived. On the other hand, the task of adaptation of a program to slightly changed specifications may often be solved by following a primarily bottom-up approach.

In both approaches, the development leads to programs with an inherent *structure* (as opposed to amorphous linear sequences of statements or instructions). It is extremely important that the goal language clearly mirror this structure. Only then is the end product a purposeful formulation, allowing systematic verification and providing insight into its history of development. But unstructured formulation, as represented in the extreme by the mass of binary digits in a computer store, is a product bare of the information that alone enables the human mind to distinguish a message from noise.

If an unfinished program is decomposed into subroutines, then the introduction of new variables often becomes necessary to represent the results and arguments of the subroutines, thereby establishing communication between the subroutines. Such variables should be understood and expressed as belonging to the development step that made them necessary. Furthermore, the refinement of the specifications of a process may have to be accompanied by a refinement in the specification of the structure of used variables. The target language should therefore be able to express data as hierarchical structures, too. The important role of the concepts of procedures, locality of objects, and structuring of data should be viewed in this wide context of systematic, stepwise program development.

The four examples that follow are supposed to illustrate these rather abstract deliberations. They do not—perhaps with the exception of the first —represent problems ordinarily encountered in data processing. They are well suited, however, to applying and demonstrating the method of stepwise development in a purposeful manner without constructing programs that are unduly long and complex. Nevertheless, the amount of text necessary to describe their careful development is a strong reminder that the construction of algorithms is far from trivial.

15.1   SOLVING A SYSTEM OF LINEAR EQUATIONS

Assume that a program is developed to compute the unknown values $x_1, \ldots, x_n$ of the system of linear equations

$$\sum_{j=1}^{n} a_{ij} * x_j = b_i \qquad i = 1, \ldots, n \tag{15.1}$$

if all a_{ij} and b_i are given. An example of such a system with $n = 3$ is

$$
\begin{aligned}
x_1 + 2 * x_2 + 5 * x_3 &= 4 \\
3 * x_1 + x_2 + 4 * x_3 &= 11 \\
-2 * x_1 + 5 * x_2 + 9 * x_3 &= -7
\end{aligned}
\tag{15.2}
$$

From the various methods of solution, we choose the one developed and extensively used (without computer) by *C. F. Gauss*: the method of successive elimination of unknowns. In the first step, we express the first unknown x_1 in terms of equation (15.1) with $i = 1$.

$$x_1 = \left(b_1 - \sum_{j=2}^{n} a_{1j} * x_j \right) \Big/ a_{11} \tag{15.3}$$

Then x_1 is substituted in the remaining $n - 1$ equations, thereby obtaining a system of $n - 1$ linear equations with the $n - 1$ unknowns $x_2, \ldots, x_n$. This process is called an *elimination step*. If it is repeated $n - 1$ times, a reduced system of one equation with one unknown is obtained, and it is easily solved.

To derive a program expressing this process more precisely, we first formulate the kth elimination step in a general form. Given is a system of $n - k + 1$ linear equations.

$$\sum_{j=k}^{n} a_{ij}^{(k)} * x_j = b_i^{(k)} \qquad i = k, \ldots, n \tag{15.4}$$

From this system, new coefficients $a_{ij}^{(k+1)}$ and $b_i^{(k+1)}$ are computed such that they form a system of $n - k$ equations.

$$\sum_{j=k+1}^{n} a_{ij}^{(k+1)} * x_j = b_i^{(k+1)} \qquad i = k+1, \ldots, n \tag{15.5}$$

These coefficients are obtained from linear combinations of the kth and the ith equations (rows), specifically

$$\begin{aligned} a_{ij}^{(k+1)} &= a_{ij}^{(k)} - (a_{kj}^{(k)} / a_{kk}^{(k)}) * a_{ik}^{(k)} \\ b_i^{(k+1)} &= b_i^{(k)} - (b_k^{(k)} / a_{kk}^{(k)}) * a_{ik}^{(k)} \end{aligned} \tag{15.6}$$

for $i, j = k + 1, \ldots, n$. The kth equation is subtracted from the ith equation after being multiplied by a factor chosen such that for $j = k$ and all i

$$a_{ik}^{(k+1)} = a_{ik}^{(k)} - (a_{kk}^{(k)} / a_{kk}^{(k)}) * a_{ik}^{(k)} = 0 \tag{15.7}$$

This means precisely that in the new system, all coefficients of the unknown x_k are zero, thus effectively eliminating x_k. Note that it is therefore unnecessary to actually compute the coefficients $a_{ik}^{(k+1)}$.

After $n - 1$ steps, the reduced system

$$a_{nn}^{(n)} * x_n = b_n^{(n)} \tag{15.8}$$

emerges from which x_n can be determined immediately. The remaining unknowns are computed by substituting the already obtained unknowns in the previously computed equations. For instance, x_{n-1} is obtained by substituting x_n in

$$a_{n-1,n-1}^{(n-1)} * x_{n-1} + a_{n-1,n}^{(n-1)} * x_n = b_{n-1}^{(n-1)} \tag{15.9}$$

This process is called a *back-substitution step*. The kth step is expressed in the general form

$$x_k = \left(b_i^{(k)} - \sum_{j=k+1}^{n} a_{ij}^{(k)} * x_j \right) \Big/ a_{ik}^{(k)} \tag{15.10}$$

for arbitrary i such that $k \leq i \leq n$. (For reasons that will be apparent later, $i = k$ is usually selected.) Observe, however, that the sequence in which the back-substitution steps are executed is fixed by the fact that for the computation of x_k, the values $x_{k+1}, \ldots, x_n$ must be known.

This entire solution process is demonstrated by using example (15.1). The equations are represented by their coefficients, written in the form of a matrix.

Elimination:

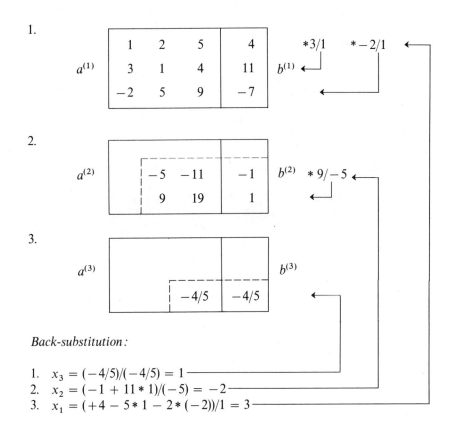

Back-substitution:

1. $x_3 = (-4/5)/(-4/5) = 1$
2. $x_2 = (-1 + 11 * 1)/(-5) = -2$
3. $x_1 = (+4 - 5 * 1 - 2 * (-2))/1 = 3$

To design a suitable program expressing this process, the recognition of one property of the described algorithm is decisive: when computing the coefficients $a^{(k+1)}$ and $b^{(k+1)}$, only coefficients $a^{(h)}$ and $b^{(h)}$ with $h = k$ are needed—none are needed with $h < k$. Is it possible, therefore, to use only two variables A and B to represent all $a^{(k)}$ and $b^{(k)}$? To answer this question, we must investigate which coefficients are significant in the later back-substitution steps. But there we have already seen that any equation with index $i = k, \ldots, n$ may be used. If the kth is chosen ($i = k$) to compute x_k, then exactly those rows of A and B that contain the coefficients $a_{ij}^{(k)}$ and $b_i^{(k)}$ for $i = k + 1, \ldots, n$ are freely available, and they may be replaced by $a_{ij}^{(k+1)}$

and $b_i^{(k+1)}$, respectively. It follows that precisely one A and one B are sufficient to represent successively the coefficients $a_{ij}^{(1)}, a_{ij}^{(2)}, \ldots, a_{ij}^{(n)}$ and $b_i^{(1)}, \ldots,$ $b_i^{(n)}$. The amount of storage needed is thereby reduced from

$$ n^2 + (n-1)^2 + \cdots + 2^2 + 1^2 = \frac{1}{6}(2n^3 + 3n^2 + n) $$

units of storage for $a^{(1)}, \ldots, a^{(n)}$ and

$$ n + (n-1) + \cdots + 2 + 1 = \tfrac{1}{2}(n^2 + n) $$

units of storage for $b^{(1)}, \ldots, b^{(n)}$ to a mere $n^2 + n$ units for both A and B. In most cases, this saving is of decisive importance and is also the key to making the Gaussian method of elimination economically applicable to available computers. (Note that similar considerations reveal that the values x_j and b_i could also share storage, thus making the introduction of a variable X unnecessary.)

Following these considerations, we declare

> **var** A: **array** $[1 \ldots n, 1 \ldots n]$ **of** *real*;
> B, X: **array** $[1 \ldots n]$ **of** *real*   (15.11)

and formulate the program

VERSION 1:   **begin** "assignment of values to A and B";
  for $k := 1$ **to** $n-1$ **do**   (15.12)
    begin "compute $a^{(k+1)}$ and $b^{(k+1)}$ from $a^{(k)}$ and $b^{(k)}$
      according to (15.6)"
    end;
  $k := n$;
  repeat "compute x_k according to (15.10)";
    $k := k - 1$
  until $k = 0$
end

Version 2 is obtained by refining the statement "compute . . . (15.6)" and may be described as

VERSION 2:   **for** $i := k+1$ **to** n **do**
  begin "compute the ith row of $a^{(k+1)}$ and $b^{(k+1)}$ according to
    (15.6)"
  end   (15.13)

At this point, it should be observed that for the computation of $a_{ij}^{(k+1)}$ (and $b_i^{(k+1)}$) according to (15.6), the factor $a_{kj}^{(k)}/a_{kk}^{(k)}$ ($b_k^{(k)}/a_{kk}^{(k)}$, respectively) is independent of the controlled variable i. Obeying the basic rule that the repeated evaluation of expressions whose constituents remain constant should be avoided, we extract the division by $a_{kk}^{(k)}$ from the **for** statement. But where should the resulting quotients be stored? Would it be possible to simply replace $a_{kj}^{(k)}$ and $b_k^{(k)}$ by $a_{kj}^{(k)}/a_{kk}^{(k)}$ and $b_k^{(k)}/a_{kk}^{(k)}$, respectively? Again, the influence of such a measure upon the back-substitution steps has to be investigated. But we know in general that the multiplication of all coefficients of an equation by the same factor does not change the values of the unknowns. Additionally, the division by $a_{kk}^{(k)}$ yields, in this case, a value 1 for $a_{kk}^{(k)}$ itself; therefore the division in the back-substitution step becomes superfluous. The proposed replacement is now not only admissible but even beneficial. This yields Version 3 of the elimination-step program.

VERSION 3:
$$\begin{aligned}
&\textbf{for } k := 1 \textbf{ to } n-1 \textbf{ do} \\
&\textbf{begin } p := 1/A[k,k]; \qquad\qquad\qquad\qquad\qquad (15.14) \\
&\qquad \textbf{for } j := k+1 \textbf{ to } n \textbf{ do } A[k,j] := p*A[k,j]; \\
&\qquad B[k] := p*B[k]; \\
&\qquad \textbf{for } i := k+1 \textbf{ to } n \textbf{ do} \\
&\qquad \textbf{begin } \text{``compute } a_i^{(k+1)} \text{ and } b_i^{(+1)} \text{ according to (15.6)''} \\
&\qquad \textbf{end} \\
&\textbf{end}
\end{aligned}$$

The refinement of statement "compute . . . (15.6)" is obtained by considering that $A[k,j]$ represents the value $a_{kj}^{(k)}/a_{kk}^{(k)}$ (in the kth step).

VERSION 4:
$$\begin{aligned}
&\textbf{for } i := k+1 \textbf{ to } n \textbf{ do} \qquad\qquad\qquad\qquad\qquad (15.15) \\
&\textbf{begin for } j := k+1 \textbf{ to } n \textbf{ do } A[i,j] := A[i,j] - A[i,k]*A[k,j]; \\
&\qquad B[i] := B[i] - A[i,k]*B[k] \\
&\textbf{end}
\end{aligned}$$

Now the same process of refinement will be applied to the back-substitution phase of (15.12). It is expressed as a succession of subtractions according to (15.10). Note that the division by $a_{kk}^{(k)}$ has already been performed in the elimination phase.

VERSION 5:
$$\begin{aligned}
&\textbf{begin } t := B[k]; \qquad\qquad\qquad\qquad\qquad\qquad (15.16) \\
&\qquad \textbf{for } j := k+1 \textbf{ to } n \textbf{ do } t := t - A[k,j]*X[j]; \\
&\qquad X[k] := t \\
&\textbf{end}
\end{aligned}$$

Note that here use is made of the rule stating that the **for** statement causes no actions if the specified limit is less than the initial value of the controlled variable.

The entire program to solve a system of linear equations is now rewritten in (15.17). Observe that now n (instead of only $n - 1$) elimination steps are executed. The nth step is necessary because it contains a division of $b_n^{(n)}$ by $a_{nn}^{(n)}$.

{Solving a system of n linear equations by Gaussian elimination}

```
var i, j, k: 1 .. n;
    p, t: real;                                                    (15.17)
    A: array [1 .. n, 1 .. n] of real;
    B, X: array [1 .. n] of real;
begin {assignment of values to A and B}
    for k := 1 to n do
    begin p := 1.0/A[k, k];
        for j := k + 1 to n do A[k, j] := p * A[k, j];
        B[k] := p * B[k];
        for i := k + 1 to n do
        begin for j := k + 1 to n do
                A[i, j] := A[i, j] − A[i, k] * A[k, j];
            B[i] := B[i] − A[i, k] * B[k]
        end
    end;
    k := n;
    repeat t := B[k];
        for j := k + 1 to n do t := t − A[k, j] * X[j];
        X[k] := t; k := k − 1
    until k = 0
    {X[1] ... X[n] are the solutions}
end
```

Particular attention must be paid to the division operation, since the algorithm fails if a divisor happens to be zero. The fact is especially significant because with the use of an arithmetic with finite precision, even divisors close to zero may cause failure or at least grossly distorted results. The fact that an arbitrary permutation of rows (equations) or columns of A and B, which is performed before each elimination step, leaves the true results unchanged permits a selection of permutations such that zero divisors can (in general) be avoided. The divisors are called *pivots.* By including a pivot search (pivoting), we can select the available component $a_{ij}^{(k)}$ with the largest absolute value. Obviously, the algorithm itself thereby gains in complexity. But pivoting is generally indispensable, if satisfactory accuracy and reliability is expected. If in some elimination step no nonzero pivot candidate can be found, then the system of equations is called *singular*; that is, it has no unique solution. And if no candidate can be found that is significantly different from zero, then the system is called *ill-conditioned* [cf. (Exercise 15.2)].

A brief analysis of the algorithm shows that the innermost operation

$$A[i, j] := A[i, j] - A[i, k] * A[k, j] \qquad (15.18)$$

is executed

$$(n - 1)^2 + (n - 2)^2 + \cdots + 2^2 + 1^2 = \tfrac{1}{6}(2n^3 - 3n^2 + n) \qquad (15.19)$$

times. The amount of computation increases roughly with the third power of n.

15.2 FINDING THE LEAST NUMBER THAT IS EQUAL TO TWO DIFFERENT SUMS OF TWO NATURAL NUMBERS RAISED TO THE THIRD POWER

The solution to this problem will demonstrate the method of stepwise refinement of program specification for a selection process whose criteria are successively refined. The problem consists of finding the least number x such that

$$x = a^3 + b^3 = c^3 + d^3 \qquad (15.20)$$

where a, b, c, d are natural numbers such that $a \neq c$ and $a \neq d$.

Without reliance on deeper number theoretical knowledge, it seems sensible to look for a solution by considering candidates (in an order of increasing magnitude) and then terminating, as soon as two consecutive candidates are equal. As candidates, we choose all sums of two natural numbers raised to the third power. The first version of such a program may be expressed as

VERSION 1: $x := 2; \{2 = 1^3 + 1^3\}$
    repeat *min* $:= x$;   (15.21)
       $x :=$ "next higher sum of two powers"
    until $x = min$

The problem is thus reduced to the refinement of the statement specifying the search for the next higher candidate. To find a clue to organize this search, we recommend computing the first few members of this sequence "by hand." This method is illustrated here, using candidates that are sums of two squares instead of cubes. Table (15.22) contains such sums in an un-ordered arrangement such that $S_{ij} = i^2 + j^2$.

j	1	2	3	4	5	6	7	8	...	
i										
1	2									
2	5	8								
3	10	13	18							
4	17	20	25	32						(15.22)
5	26	29	34	41	50					
6	37	40	45	52	61	72				
7	50	53	58	65	74	85	98			
8	65	68	73	80	89	100	113	128		
9	82	85	...							
...										

The table shows that

$$50 = 1^2 + 7^2 = 5^2 + 5^2$$
$$65 = 1^2 + 8^2 = 4^2 + 7^2$$
$$85 = 2^2 + 9^2 = 6^2 + 7^2$$

and that 50 is therefore the desired least number. The principal task now is to find a search method yielding the candidates in order of increasing magnitude; that is,

$$2, 5, 8, 10, 13, 17, \ldots, 45, 50, 50$$

The following facts are useful and will determine the future developments.

1. $S_{ij} > S_{ik}$ for all i and all $j > k$.
2. $S_{ij} > S_{kj}$ for all j and all $i > k$.
3. $S_{ij} = S_{ji}$; it suffices to consider only S_{ij} with $j \leq i$.

From statement 1, it follows that it is unnecessary to store an entire row of candidates at any one time; it suffices to proceed in each line from left to right and to retain the last candidate generated. Consequently, the table may be represented by the variable

var S: **array** $[1 .. ?]$ **of** *integer*   (15.23)

To facilitate the computation of the next candidate in a row, a further variable

var j: **array** $[1 .. ?]$ **of** *integer*   (15.24) is introduced such that its kth element represents the index of the last generated candidate in the kth row of the table; that is,

$$S[k] = k^3 + j[k]^3 \tag{15.25}$$

If the index i of the last considered candidate is used instead of the candidate x itself and if a function $p(k) = k^3$ is introduced, then a second version of the program may be formulated.

VERSION 2: $i := 1$;
        for $k := 1$ **to** ? **do**
           begin $j[k] := 1$; $S[k] := p(k) + 1$ (15.26)
           end;
        repeat $min := S[i]$;
          1: "increment $j[i]$ and replace $S[i]$ by the next candidate in the ith row"
          2: "determine a new value of i as the index of the row with the least candidate"
        until $S[i] = min$

This version is unacceptable as a final solution because an indefinite number of components $S[k]$ have to be initialized with $k^3 + 1^3$. Furthermore, statement 2 implies a selection among an indefinite number of candidates. However, if we consider condition 2, then selection (and initialization) may be restricted to components $S[k]$ with $k \leq ih$, if ih is defined as the least index such that $j[ih] = 1$ (i.e., $j[k] > 1$ for all $k < ih$). These considerations lead to

VERSION 3: $i := 1$; $ih := 2$;   (15.27)
        $j[1] := 1$; $S[1] := 2$; $j[2] := 1$; $S[2] := p(2) + 1$;
        repeat $min := S[i]$;
          1: **if** $j[i] = 1$ **then** "increment ih and initialize $S[ih]$"
          2: "increment $j[i]$ and replace $S[i]$ by the next candidate in row i"
          3: "determine i such that $S[i] = min(S[1] \ldots S[ih])$"
        until $S[i] = min$

During a further refinement of the three labeled statements, keep in mind that generation of candidates (in row i) must be terminated as soon as $j[i] = i$. This is advantageous because the symmetry of the table of candidates allows for a limitation of the search to its lower left triangle, and it is also necessary because otherwise pairs of values $a^3 + b^3$ and $b^3 + a^3$ would be generated and recognized as equal. The fact that indices $j[i]$ may reach a limit—thus effectively eliminating the ith row from a further search—makes the introduction of a lower limit of the row index i necessary; we call it il. The selection of candidates is thereby further restricted in a most desirable way to rows with indices between il and ih. il is incremented whenever a row is eliminated.

VERSION 4: $i := 1; il := 1; ih := 2; \ldots$ (15.28)

        repeat $min := S[i]$;

           if $j[i] = i$ **then** $il := il + 1$ **else**

                begin 1: **if** $j[i] = 1$ **then**

                        "increment ih and initialize $S[ih]$"

                     2: "increment $j[i]$ and replace $S[i] \ldots$"

                end;

           3: "determine i such that $S[i] = min(S[il] \ldots S[ih])$"

        until $S[i] = min$

Subsequently, statements labeled 1–3 have to be further refined. If, in statement 3, min is determined by a simple linear search among $S_{il}, \ldots, S_{ih}$ [cf. (11.19)], then we obtain the following partial program.

        3: $i := il; k := i$;

          while $k < ih$ **do**   (15.29)

          begin $\{S[i] = min(S[il] \ldots S[k])\}$ $k := k + 1$;

             if $S[k] < S[i]$ **then** $i := k$

          end

Likewise, statements 2 and 1 can be formulated in a straightforward manner.

        2: $j[i] := j[i] + 1$; $S[i] := p(i) + p(j[i])$ (15.30)

        1: **if** $j[i] = 1$ **then**

          begin $ih := ih + 1$; $j[ih] := 1$; $S[ih] := p(ih) + 1$ (15.31)

          end

The program thus obtained may now be further improved, if the repeated evaluation of $p(i)$ to compute the sums $S[i]$ is avoided. Such an improvement is easy to realize because a new third power has to be computed when and only when ih is incremented. This fact facilitates significantly the incorporation of such a refinement. The computed powers are represented by a variable

          var p: **array** $[1 .. ?]$ **of** $integer$ (15.32)

and the function designators $p(i)$ are merely replaced by $p[i]$. The only amendment to the existing program is the inclusion of

          $p[ih] := ih * ih * ih$ (15.33)

in statement 1 in (15.31).

These considerations lead to the final complete version of the program, shown in (15.34). This program determines the desired least number as

$$1729 = 10^3 + 9^3 = 12^3 + 1^3$$

after examining 61 candidates. The final index limits are $il = 10$ and $ih = 12$, and the relation $S[k] < S[i]$ is evaluated 107 times.

```
var i, il, ih, min, a, b, k: integer;                              (15.34)
    j, p, S: array [1 .. 12] of integer;
    {p[k] = k³, S[k] = p[k] + p[j[k]] for  k = 1 ... ih}
begin i := 1; il := 1; ih := 2;
    j[1] := 1; p[1] := 1; S[1] := 2; j[2] := 1; p[2] := 8; S[2] := 9;
    repeat min := S[i]; a := i; b := j[i];
        if j[i] = i then il := il + 1 else
        begin if j[i] = 1 then
            begin ih := ih + 1; p[ih] := ih * ih * ih;
                  j[ih] := 1; S[ih] := p[ih] + 1
            end;
            j[i] := j[i] + 1; S[i] := p[i] + p[j[i]]
        end;
        i := il; k := i;
        while k < ih do
            begin k := k + 1;
                  if S[k] < S[i] then i := k
            end
    until S[i] = min;
    writeIn(min, a, b, i, j[i])
end.
```

By changing the expression in (15.33) and some initial values of S and p, the same program may also be used to compute the least number representable as two different sums of two fourth powers. However, the necessary amount of computation increases drastically. The result is obtained as

$$634318657 = 134^4 + 133^4 = 158^4 + 59^4$$

after examining 11660 candidates.

15.3 DETERMINE THE FIRST n PRIME NUMBERS

As in the previous section, a program designed to find the first n prime numbers has to scan the set of natural numbers in ascending order and then select members meeting certain criteria. In this case, the condition for termination is even simpler, and one is inclined to immediately propose the following program.

VERSION 1:   **var** i, x: *integer*;   (15.35)
                 begin $x := 1$;
                    for $i := 1$ **to** n **do**
                        begin $x :=$ "next prime number"; *write*(x)
                      end
        end.

The only statement that needs further refinement is "$x :=$ next prime number." It is also the only one referring to the fact that we are to generate prime numbers instead of any other kind of numbers. Introducing a Boolean variable *prim*, it can be expressed as

VERSION 2:   **repeat** $x := x + 1$;   (15.36)
                prim $:=$ "x is a prime number"
        until *prim*

Considering the fact that with the exception of the first, all prime numbers are odd, the computational effort can quickly be halved. If the number 2 is treated as a special case, then x can be incremented in steps of 2. The next task is to refine the statement

$$prim := \text{``}x \text{ is a prime number''}$$

We must therefore take into account the definition of a prime number: x is prime if and only if x is divisible only by 1 and itself, that is, if division by $2, 3, \ldots, x - 1$ always yields a nonzero remainder. This successive testing dictates a further iteration, yielding a nested repetitive statement structure.

VERSION 3:   **repeat** $x := x + 2; k := 2$;   (15.37)
                repeat {x is not divisible by $2, 3 \ldots k$}
                    $k := k + 1$; *prim* $:=$ "x is not divisible by k"
                until $\neg prim \lor (k \geq lim)$
        until *prim*

Obviously, the limiting value for k may be taken as $lim = x - 1$. But it is sufficient and more economical to choose $lim = \sqrt{x}$, since if x were divisible by a number $k > \sqrt{x}$, then x could be expressed as $x = k * j$, which implies that x would also be divisible by $j < \sqrt{x}$. But this has already been proved not to be the case.

Equally decisive in the further development of the algorithm and the saving of computational effort is the recognition of the fact that it is perfectly sufficient to test divisibility of x by prime numbers only. For if x were divisible by a nonprime k, then it would also be divisible by the prime factors of k. It therefore appears wise to retain the already computed prime numbers in a table p, where p_k is the kth prime number. Taking these developments into account, we obtain

VERSION 4:   **repeat** $x := x + 2$; $k := 2$; $prim := true$;
    while $prim \wedge (k < lim)$ **do**   (15.38)
    begin $prim :=$ "x is not divisible by $p[k]$"
      $k := k + 1$
    end
   until $prim$;
   $p[i] := x$

We now have to redetermine the value lim as the *index* of the largest prime number for which divisibility has to be tested, so that

$$p[lim] > \sqrt{x} \quad \text{and} \quad p[lim - 1] \leq \sqrt{x} \qquad (15.39)$$

So far, we always assumed that the values $p_1, \ldots, p_{lim}$ were known, that is, previously computed. But this condition will be satisfied only if the candidate x to be tested is always less than p^2_{lim}, that is if, in every instance,

$$p[i] < p[i - 1]^2 \qquad (15.40)$$

Fortunately, this relation is one of the deeper results of number theory and holds for all prime numbers. We note that the index lim has to be redetermined whenever x is incremented and also has to be increased whenever $p^2_{lim} \leq x$. Increasing of lim by 1 is sufficient because x had been incremented by only 2 since the last test and because $p^2_{i+1} > p^2_i + 2$ for all i. These considerations lead to version 5—written as a complete program—which summarizes the developments made so far.

VERSION 5:   **type** $index = 1 .. n$;
   var x: *integer*;
    i, k, lim: *index*; $prim$: *Boolean*;
    p: **array** $[index]$ **of** *integer*; $\{p[i] = i$th prime number$\}$
   begin $p[1] := 2$; $write(2)$; $x := 1$; $lim := 1$;
    for $i := 2$ **to** n **do**
    begin
      repeat $x := x + 2$;
       if $sqr(p[lim]) \leq x$ **then** $lim := lim + 1$;
       $k := 2$; $prim := true$;   (15.41)

$$\textbf{while } prim \wedge (k < lim) \textbf{ do}$$
$$\textbf{begin } prim := \text{``}x \text{ is not divisible by } p[k]\text{''};$$
$$k := k + 1$$
$$\textbf{end}$$
$$\textbf{until } prim;$$
$$p[i] := x; \; write(x)$$
$$\textbf{end}$$
$$\textbf{end.}$$

Finally, the statement

$$prim := \text{``}x \text{ is not divisible by } p[k]\text{''}$$

must be subjected to further refinements. With the operators introduced in Section 8.1, the above statement can easily be expressed as either

$$prim := (x \bmod p[k]) \neq 0 \qquad (15.42.1)$$

or

$$prim := (x \textbf{ div } p[k]) * p[k] \neq x \qquad (15.42.2)$$

This may well be regarded as the final step in the construction of a program to find prime numbers. Let us, however, assume that the program is to be developed without the availability of an explicit division operator. In this case, the stepwise refinement process has to be carried on further. Obviously, division may be replaced by a sequence of subtractions and expressed by another repetitive statement.

$$r := x; \qquad\qquad\qquad\qquad\qquad (15.43)$$
$$\textbf{repeat } r := r - p[k] \textbf{ until } r \leq 0;$$
$$prim := r < 0$$

However, since this statement will be executed rather frequently and the process of repeated subtraction may therefore be rather costly, it seems to be particularly appropriate to look for potentially more economical solutions. One appropriate and at the same time simple solution consists of tabulating not only the prime numbers $p_1, \ldots, p_{lim}$ but also their multiples $V_k = m * p_k$ such that

$$x \leq V[k] < x + p[k] \quad \text{for } k = 2, \ldots, lim \qquad (15.44)$$

In this case, the divisibility of x by p_k may simply be determined by comparison of x with V_k. If—with due respect to the extremely frequent evaluation of p_{lim}^2—we introduce an auxiliary variable called *square* whose value is

$$square = p[lim]^2 \qquad (15.45)$$

then we will obtain the final version of the program.†

† E. W. Dijkstra, "Structured programming", EWD249, T. H. Eindhoven (1969).

VERSION 6:   **type** *index* = 1 .. *n*;
              var *x*, *square*: *integer*;
                 i, *k*, *lim*: *index*; *prim*: *Boolean*;
                 p: **array** [*index*] **of** *integer*;
                 V: **array** [1 .. $\sqrt{n}$] **of** *integer*;
              begin *p*[1] := 2; *write*(2); *x* := 1; *lim* := 1; *square* := 4;
                 for *i* := 2 **to** *n* **do**
                 begin
                    repeat *x* := *x* + 2;
                       if *square* ≤ *x* **then**   (15.46)
                          begin *V*[*lim*] := *square*;
                             lim := *lim* + 1; *square* := *sqr*(*p*[*lim*])
                          end;
                       k := 2; *prim* := *true*;
                       while *prim* ∧ (*k* < *lim*) **do**
                          begin if *V*[*k*] < *x* **then**
                                   V[*k*] := *V*[*k*] + *p*[*k*];   •
                                   prim := (*x* ≠ *V*[*k*]); *k* := *k* + 1
                          end
                    until *prim*;
                    p[*i*] := *x*; *write*(*x*)
                 end
              end.

This example clearly demonstrates that by being forced to work with a simpler tool (a computer without built-in division), the programmer is given the incentive to look for a solution that ultimately turns out to be superior. It is not uncommon to find that the availability of very powerful computers with large stores discourages programmers from refining their algorithms to the most suitable, pertinent, and economical version.

The following table shows the frequency of execution of the four different statements in (15.46), depending on the number *n* of prime numbers to be computed.

n =	10	20	50	500	1000
x := *x* + 2	14	114	611	1785	3959
lim := *lim* + 1	3	6	11	17	23
prim := (*x* ≠ *V*[*k*])	13	268	2340	9099	25133
V[*k*] := *V*[*k*] + *p*[*k*]	8	156	1151	3848	9287

(15.47)

15.4 A HEURISTIC ALGORITHM

The program developed in this section is a simple but typical example of a class of algorithms that determine a solution not in a straightforward manner but in a heuristic fashion—that is, by trying, checking, and retrying. The essential characteristic of the heuristic method is that candidates for a solution are generated stepwise according to a given pattern; then they are subjected to tests according to the criteria characterizing the solution. If a candidate turns out to be unacceptable, then another candidate is generated in which case several steps previously undertaken may have to be annulled. The task of the algorithm to be designed is:

Generate a sequence of N characters, chosen from an alphabet of three elements (e.g., 1, 2, 3), such that no two immediately adjacent subsequences are equal.

For instance, the sequence of length $N = 5$ with the characters "12321" is acceptable, but neither "12323" nor "12123" are.

If one is confronted with a problem of this kind, it is advisable to let a sequence of length N grow systematically (starting with the empty sequence) by appending one character in each step. Since there is no sense in letting a sequence grow that does not meet the criteria, the logical consequence is to test the sequence in each step and to append a character if it meets the stated criteria—otherwise change the sequence. In the first version of the program, we introduce one variable each to denote the length and the quality of the sequence constructed so far. The former is of type *integer* and is denoted as m; the latter may either be defined over a range of two values *good* and *bad* or be declared of type *Boolean* and given an appropriate name. The two possibilities are

$$\textbf{var } q: (good, bad)$$
and
$$\textbf{var } good: Boolean$$

We choose the second option with the meanings

> *good* = *true*: the sequence satisfies the condition
> *good* = *false*: the sequence does not satisfy the condition

Thus we formulate

VERSION 1:
```
var m: 0 .. N;   good: Boolean;   S: Sequence;          (15.48)
begin m := 0; good := true; {the empty sequence is good}
      repeat if good then "extend the sequence S"
                     else "change the sequence S"
             good := "S is a good sequence"
      until good ∧ (m = N);
      print(S)
end.
```

Change here means the alteration of certain components or their removal, but no increase in the length of the sequence. In order to guarantee termination, changes must be performed in such a manner that a sequence that once was determined as not *good* will never be generated again. This implies that the changes must be made according to a systematic pattern and that among the possible candidates there exists a certain ordering, which is followed during the process of generating them. The above choice of names for the three characters (namely, 1, 2, and 3) already suggests a possible ordering: if a sequence $S = s_1 s_2 s_3 \ldots$ is considered as a decimal fraction with value $|S| = 0.s_1 s_2 \ldots$, then the ordering relation $\prec$ is defined by

$$S \prec S' \quad \leftrightarrow \quad |S| < |S'| \tag{15.49}$$

Now the algorithms for changing and extending a sequence are essentially determined too. An extension must be chosen such that it represents the least possible candidate so that a possible later change will never cause any candidate to be left unconsidered. Assuming the ordering '1' $\prec$ '2' $\prec$ '3', every extension must always append a '1'.

To describe the two operations in more detail and in terms of statements in our programming language, it is necessary to refine further the description of the structure of the variable S. Because its components are continually reinspected and even altered, the file structure must be dismissed immediately as inappropriate. The declaration is therefore

$$\textbf{var } S\text{: } \textbf{array } [1 \ldots N] \textbf{ of } char \tag{15.50}$$

When specifying the details of the operation *change*, remember that the component $S[m]$ cannot be blindly replaced by its successor value. If $S[m] = $ '3', there is no successor. This is exactly a case in which the sequence must be shortened. The second to the last component, however, may again have the value '3'. The action of shortening the sequence and, in general, of giving up an attempted solution is called *backtracking*. The reader is encouraged to try to generate candidates by himself using this algorithm. The first ten are shown in (15.51), where the acceptable ones are marked with a + sign.

$$
\begin{array}{l}
+ \;\; 1 \\
 \;\; 11 \\
+ \;\; 12 \\
+ \;\; 121 \\
 \;\; 1211 \\
 \;\; 1212 \\
+ \;\; 1213 \\
+ \;\; 12131 \\
 \;\; 121311 \\
+ \;\; 121312 \\
 \;\; \cdots
\end{array}
\tag{15.51}
$$

If we formulate the operations of extending, changing, and checking a sequence as procedures, the resulting program is

VERSION 2:   **var** S: **array** $[1 .. N]$ **of** $char$;
                      m: $0 .. N$; $good$: $Boolean$;
              procedure $extend$;   (15.52)
                      begin $m := m + 1$; $S[m] := '1'$ **end**;
              procedure $change$;
                      begin if $S[m] < '3'$ **then** $S[m] := succ(S[m])$ **else**
                              begin $m := m - 1$; {shorten S}
                                      if $m > 0$ **then**
                                      if $S[m] < '3'$ **then** $S[m] := succ(S[m])$ **else**
                                      begin $m := m - 1$; {empty sequence}
                                              if $m > 0$ **then** $S[m] := succ(S[m])$
                                      end
                              end
                      end;
              begin $m := 0$; $good := true$;
                      repeat if $good$ **then** $extend$ **else** $change$;
                      $check$
                      until $good \land (m = N) \lor (m = 0)$;
                      $print(S)$
              end.

This version takes into account the possibility that a truncation of S may lead to a zero length sequence by including the term $m = 0$ in the termination condition. Furthermore, it is noteworthy that the procedure $change$ provides for a shortening of S by at most 2 components. This is permissible because the proposed candidates are always generated by appending a single character to a $good$ sequence (which may never contain two adjacent equal characters).

Before proceeding with the program's refinement process, a variant of the current version should be considered that embodies a slightly more efficient solution. We note first of all that the three operations $extend$, $change$, and $check$ always alternate according to the following pattern.

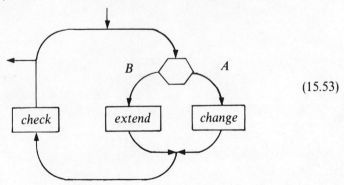

(15.53)

It is to be expected that path A will be selected more frequently than path B. Version 2′ allows the repetition of *change* to be formulated with a slightly simpler termination condition, making use of a nested statement structure.

VERSION 2′:   **repeat** *extend*; *check*;
                   while ¬ *good* ∧ (*m* > 0) **do**   (15.54)
                        begin *change*; *check* **end**
                 until (*m* = *N*) ∨ (*m* = 0)

This variant of Version 2 corresponds to pattern (15.55), which shows that the possible sequences of operations are the same as in (15.53).

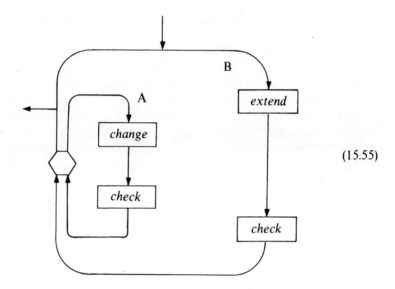

(15.55)

Looking at the complete Version 2, it is primarily the complexity of the operation *change* and the termination conditions that is disturbing. The former, however, can be reduced by a fairly common "trick." The complexity of *change* stems from its consideration of a situation that occurs rarely if ever: the reduction of *S* to the empty sequence. In this case, an assignment to the nonexisting element *S*[0] must be prevented. The "trick" consists of introducing a dummy component *S*[0] and admitting a possible assignment to *S*[0]. The procedure *change* may then be simplified to

    procedure *change*;
     begin while $S[m] = $ '3' **do** $m := m - 1$;
      $S[m] := succ(S[m])$ (15.56)
     end

If, however, the existence of a desired sequence of length *N* is assured— possibly on the basis of combinatorial analysis—then (15.56) may be used even without an element $S[0]$, and the main program (15.54) may be further simplified to

$$\begin{aligned}
&\textbf{repeat } \textit{extend}; \textit{ check}; \\
&\qquad \textbf{while } \neg \textit{ good } \textbf{do} \\
&\qquad\qquad \textbf{begin } \textit{change}; \textit{ check } \textbf{end} \\
&\textbf{until } m = N
\end{aligned} \qquad (15.57)$$

The entire program is now formulated in the target programming language with the exception of the operation *check*, whose definition [cf. (15.48)] is given as

$$good := \text{``}S \text{ is an acceptable sequence''}$$

It is noteworthy that up to this point, no reference has been made to the criteria that characterize a solution. (Use was merely made of the property that no solutions could be obtained by extending unacceptable sequences). But this means that the program developed so far is of *considerable generality*.

In the posed problem, the procedure *check* has to determine whether S is free of equal adjacent sub-sequences. The sub-sequences to be compared vary in length from 1 to $m/2$. Since a comparison of two sequences of length L requires L comparisons of characters, the total number of elementary comparisons is (at most)

$$N(m) = (m-1)*1 + (m-3)*2 + \cdots + 3*(m/2 - 1) + 1*(m/2)$$

$$= \frac{1}{24}(m^3 + 3*m^2 + 2*m) \qquad (15.58)$$

for even m and

$$N(m) = (m-1)*1 + (m-3)*2 + \cdots + 4*\left(\frac{m-3}{2}\right) + 2*\left(\frac{m-1}{2}\right)$$

$$= \frac{1}{24}(m^3 + 3*m^2 - m - 3) \qquad (15.59)$$

for odd m. For large m, $N(m)$ apparently grows with the third power of m and makes the usefulness of this program doubtful. However, its effectiveness can be drastically improved after some further deliberations. Every candidate S was generated by appending a single element to a sequence certified as *good*. Consequently, it suffices to compare only those adjacent sub-sequences that include the last appended character, that is, all pairs

$$\langle S_{m-2L+1} \cdots S_{m-L}, \; S_{m-L+1} \cdots S_m \rangle \qquad (15.60)$$

with $L = 1, \ldots, m/2$. The (maximum) number of elementary comparisons thus reduces to

$$N(m) = 1 + 2 + \cdots + \frac{m}{2} = \tfrac{1}{8}(m^2 + 2m) \qquad (15.61)$$

According to these considerations, the procedure *check* may be formulated as follows

> **procedure** *check*;
>   **var** L: *integer*;
> **begin** *good* := *true*;   (15.62)
>   **for** $L := 1$ **to** (m **div** 2) **do**
>   *good* := *good* $\wedge$ $((S_{m-2L+1} \cdots S_{m-L}) \neq (S_{m-L+1} \cdots S_m))$
> **end**

But a more efficient variant is obtained by doing what is obvious; terminating comparisons as soon as two sub-sequences are recognized as equal. [Note that, in general, program schema (9.2) should not be adopted unchanged whenever the recurrence relation $v_i = f(v_{i-1})$ assumes the form $v_i = (v_{i-1} \wedge q_i)$.] The improved version of (15.62) is shown in (15.63). Since the number of necessary repetitions is no longer known beforehand, the **for** statement is replaced by a **while** structure.

> **procedure** *check*;
>   **var** L, *mhalf*: *integer*;   (15.63)
> **begin** *good* := *true*; $L := 0$; *mhalf* := m **div** 2;
>   **while** *good* $\wedge$ $(L < mhalf)$ **do**
>   **begin** $L := L + 1$;
>   *good* := $(S_{m-2L+1} \cdots S_{m-L}) \neq (S_{m-L+1} \cdots S_m)$
>   **end**
> **end**

By using the same principle—this time applying a repeat clause, since all sub-sequences consist of at least one character—the comparison of sequences of characters is replaced by a sequence of comparisons of characters. (15.64) shows the final version of the procedure *check*. All operations are now formulated in terms of our basic programming notation.

> **procedure** *check*;
>   **var** i, L, *mhalf*: *integer*;   (15.64)
> **begin** *good* := *true*; $L := 0$; *mhalf* := m **div** 2;
>   **while** *good* $\wedge$ $(L < mhalf)$ **do**
>   **begin** $L := L + 1$; $i := 0$;
>   **repeat** *good* := $S[m-i] \neq S[m-L-i]$; $i := i + 1$
>   **until** *good* $\vee$ $(i = L)$
>   **end**
> **end**

The initially posed problem is now completely solved, as described in (15.52), (15.56), (15.57), and (15.64).

Finally, we will use the problem of nonrepeating sub-sequences as an example to illustrate a practical situation that occurs quite frequently: the original problem is either extended or slightly modified. Consequently, the existing program has to be *adapted*.

The problem extension to be considered in our example is:

> *Instead of a single, arbitrary sequence of length N, find* all *sequences of length N that contain no equal adjacent sub-sequences.*

Fortunately, the program developed is sufficiently partitioned so that many of the individual parts may be retained unaltered. In general, the more clearly and appropriately a program is structured, the easier its adaptation to slightly changed tasks—it is simpler to isolate the components that have to undergo a modification. In the present case, not only the clear decomposition of the program but also the systematic principle of generating candidates turn out to be most beneficial. The following considerations lead to an immediate solution [cf. (15.52)].

1. If m reaches N, then S is recognized as a result and is printed. Subsequently, it is subjected to a change rather than an extension.
2. The condition for termination can be simplified because the relation $m = N$ is no longer relevant. Only the term $m = 0$ is retained.

The reader is urged to convince himself that the resulting algorithm issues only acceptable sequences and that it does generate all possible solutions. (15.65) shows the generated candidates for the case $N = 3$; solutions are marked with a + sign.

1	2	3	
12	21	31	
+ 121	+ 212	+ 312	
+ 123	+ 213	+ 313	(15.65)
13	23	32	
+ 131	+ 231	+ 321	
+ 132	+ 232	+ 323	

From this table, it is apparent that among the 12 solutions several are similar in the sense that they can be obtained from each other by cyclic permutation of the basic characters.

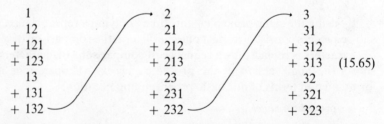

$$(15.66)$$

Actually, there are only two significantly different solutions, represented by "123" and "121." A program that generates only a single member of every group of 6 similar solutions is obtained by terminating the generating process as soon as an attempt is made to change $S[2]$. (Consequently, the dummy component $S[0]$ is not needed here either.) Thus we obtain the final solution of the extended problem, presented in (15.67) as a complete program.

```
var S: array [1 .. N] of char;
    m: integer;  good: Boolean;
procedure extend;                                    (15.67)
    begin m := m + 1; S[m] := '1' end;
procedure change;
    begin {cf. (15.56)} end;
procedure check;
    begin {cf. (15.64)} end;
procedure print;
    var i: integer;
    begin for i := 1 to N do write(S[i]);
        writeIn
    end;
begin m := 2; S[1] := '1'; S[2] := '2'; good := true;
    repeat if good then
                if m = N then begin print; change end
                else extend
            else change;
            check
    until m = 2
end.
```

Table (15.68) shows the number K of solutions as a function of their length N. The reduction factor 6 is already incorporated.

N	$K(N)$	N	$K(N)$	N	$K(N)$
3	2	9	18	15	103
4	3	10	24	16	133
5	5	11	34	17	174
6	7	12	44	18	232
7	10	13	57	19	305
8	13	14	76	20	398

(15.68)

EXERCISES

15.1 The program to solve a system of linear equations given in (15.17) can be simplified, if the variable B is represented as an additional column of matrix A; that is,

$$
A = \begin{pmatrix}
a_{11} & a_{12} & \cdots & a_{1n} & b_1 \\
a_{21} & a_{22} & \cdots & a_{2n} & b_2 \\
\cdots & & & & \cdots \\
a_{n1} & a_{n2} & \cdots & a_{nn} & b_n
\end{pmatrix}
$$

Write the corresponding program incorporating all ensuing simplifications. (Note that both programs represent the same algorithm.)

15.2 Extend program (15.17) to solve a system of linear equations so that it includes *pivoting*.

Variant 1: In the kth elimination step, select as the pivot the element $a_{hk}^{(k)}$ with the largest absolute value in the kth column (*column pivoting*); that is,

$$
|a_{hk}^{(k)}| \geq |a_{ik}^{(k)}| \quad \text{for } i = k, \cdots, n
$$

Hint: After determining the pivot $a_{hk}^{(k)}$, exchange rows $a_h^{(k)}$ with $a_k^{(k)}$ and also $b_h^{(k)}$ with $b_k^{(k)}$.

Variant 2: In the kth elimination step, select as the pivot the element $a_{hm}^{(k)}$ with the largest absolute value in the kth column and the kth row (*total pivoting*); that is,

$$
|a_{hm}^{(k)}| \geq |a_{ij}^{(k)}| \quad \text{for } i,j = k, \cdots, n
$$

Hint: After selecting the pivot $a_{hm}^{(k)}$, the rows $a_h^{(k)}$ and $a_k^{(k)}$ ($b_h^{(k)}$ and $b_k^{(k)}$) are interchanged. Then the columns $a_{xm}^{(k)}$ and $a_{xk}^{(k)}$ are interchanged, whereby the column interchange $\langle m, k \rangle$ has to be recorded because the latter implies a permutation of the unknowns x_m and x_k, which must be considered in the back-substitution steps. Finally, if there is no element $a_{ij}^{(k)}$ with absolute value greater than ε (choose, for example, $\varepsilon = 10^{-8}$), then the system is ill conditioned, and the program will specify an exit jump to some predefined statement [cf. (14.24)].

15.3 Extend program (15.17) to solve a system of linear equations using the following methods.

Variant 1: In the kth elimination step, all components of row $a_i^{(k)}$ are multiplied with the same *scaling factor* $s_i^{(k)}$ ($i = k, \ldots, n$). Note that the true solutions x_j are not affected by such a multiplication. However, accuracy of the computed results x_j may be improved. Choose

$$
s_i^{(k)} = 1 \bigg/ \sum_{j=k}^{n} a_{ij}^{(k)} \quad \text{for } i = k, \ldots, n
$$

Variant 2:   In the kth elimination step, all components of the jth column are multiplied with the same *scaling factor* $s_j^{(k)}$ $(j = k, \ldots, n)$. The computed results x_j must be readjusted accordingly in the back-substitution phase. Choose

$$s_j^{(k)} = 1 \Big/ \sum_{i=k}^{n} a_{ij}^{(k)} \quad \text{for } j = k, \ldots, n$$

15.4   Design a program to solve the following system of n linear equations, given the coefficients a_{ij} and b_i.

$$a_{11} * x_1 + a_{12} * x_2 = b_1$$

$$a_{k,k-1} * x_{k-1} + a_{kk} * x_k + a_{k,k+1} * x_{k+1} = b_k \quad \text{for } k = 2, \ldots, n-1$$

$$a_{n,n-1} * x_{n-1} + a_{nn} * x_n = b_n$$

If the coefficients a_{ij} are arranged in the form of a matrix, then the following *tridiagonal* form is obtained.

$$\begin{pmatrix} a_{11} & a_{12} & & & & \\ a_{21} & a_{22} & a_{23} & & 0 & \\ & a_{32} & a_{33} & a_{34} & & \\ & & \ddots & \ddots & \ddots & \\ & 0 & & & & \\ & & & & a_{n,n-1} & a_{n,n} \end{pmatrix}$$

Hint: In the kth elimination step, only the following two coefficients have to be computed.

$$a_{k+1,k+1}^{(k+1)} = a_{k+1,k+1}^{(k)} - (a_{k+1,k}^{(k)} * a_{k,k+1}^{(k)})/a_{kk}^{(k)}$$

and

$$b_{k+1}^{(k+1)} = b_{k+1}^{(k)} - (a_{k+1,k}^{(k)} * b_k^{(k)})/a_{kk}^{(k)}$$

All other coefficients remain the same. The tridiagonal matrix is represented by the array variable

var A: **array** $[1 \ldots n, -1 \ldots 1]$ **of** *real*

where the coefficients $a_{ij}^{(k)}$ are denoted as $A[i, j - i]$. In this way, coefficients that, by definition, are identical to zero, do not occupy any storage.

15.5   Develop a program to solve the following system of n linear equations.

$$\sum_{j=1}^{i} a_{ij} * x_j = b_i \quad \text{for } i = 1, \ldots, n$$

In this special case, the non-zero coefficients a_{ij} form the *triangular matrix*

$$A = \begin{pmatrix} a_{11} & & & & \\ a_{21} & a_{22} & & & 0 \\ a_{31} & a_{32} & a_{33} & & \\ \cdots\cdots\cdots\cdots\cdots & & & \\ a_{n1} & \cdots & & & a_{nn} \end{pmatrix}$$

Notice that the Gaussian algorithm of elimination may be significantly simplified and that only $\frac{1}{2}n(n + 1)$ coefficients have to be stored. The matrix a_{ij} is therefore represented by the array variable

$$A: \textbf{array } [1 \ldots m] \textbf{ of } real \qquad m = \tfrac{1}{2}n(n + 1)$$

and the coefficients a_{ij} are denoted by $A[i * (i - 1) \textbf{ div } 2 + j]$.

15.6   Extend program (15.34) in such a way that it generates not only the least but the 10 smallest numbers representable as two different sums of two third powers of natural numbers. These ten pairs of sums $\langle a_i, b_i \rangle$ are to be selected such that their terms are linearly independent; that is, there must be no multiplier n such that

$$a_i = n * a_j \quad \text{and} \quad b_i = n * b_j \qquad i \neq j$$

15.7   Consider the following program to solve the problem in Section 15.2.

```
var i, j, m, n, x: integer; p: array [0 .. 13] of integer;
begin m := 0; p[0] := 0;
    while m < 13 do
    begin m := m + 1; p[m] := m * m * m; n := 0;          (15.69)
       while n < m do
       begin n := n + 1; x := p[m] + p[n]; i := m - 1;
          {x is the next candidate}
          while 2 * p[i] > x do
          begin j := i - 1;
             while p[i] + p[j] > x do j := j - 1;
             if p[i] + p[j] = x then go to 99 else i := i - 1
          end
       end
    end;
99: write(x, m, n, i, j)
end.
```

Determine the history of development and the verification conditions on which this program is based.

Although the program computes the correct result 1729, the possibility does exist that its author has made use of a condition that is difficult to prove and that he tacitly assumed to be true. (Which one?) The program is thus an example of a correct solution obtained by incorrect reasoning.

Compare the amount of computation prescribed by this program with that in program (15.34), both altered to the case of fourth powers ($x^4 = a^4 + b^4 = c^4 + d^4$).

15.8 Design a program computing the least ten numbers x_i whose third powers are sums of three third powers.

$$x_i^3 = a_i^3 + b_i^3 + c_i^3 \quad \text{for } i = 1, \ldots, 10$$

The terms are to be linearly independent; that is, there must be no multiplier n such that for any $i \neq j$, $a_i = n * a_j$, $b_i = n * b_j$, and $c_i = n * c_j$.

15.9 Determine analytically (i.e., without the aid of a computer) the effect of changing the clause

to

if *square* $\leq x$ **then**   (15.70)

if *square* $< x$ **then**

in program (15.46).

15.10 By changing program (15.46) according to (15.70) and by changing the clause

to

while $n < lim$ **do**   (15.71)

while $n \leq lim$ **do**

the program becomes false. Which is the ignored and thereby violated invariant? Retaining the two changes, how can the program be easily corrected? Is the resulting version more or less efficient than the algorithm of (15.46)?

15.11 The conclusion

$$x \neq a \quad \leftrightarrow \quad \text{"x" is not divisible by p"}$$

in program (15.46) is justified only if the prerequisites

$$x \leq a < x + p \quad \text{and} \quad a = n * p$$

are both satisfied. Verify by insertion of the relevant assertions that these conditions are invariants of the following partial program [extracted from (15.46)], if p is a natural number greater than 2.

```
x := 1; a := 0;
repeat x := x + 2;
    if a < x then a := a + p;                    (15.72)
    {x ≤ a < x + p, a = n * p}
until P
```

15.12 Develop a program that generates in ascending order the least 100 numbers of the set M, where M is defined as follows.

(a) The number 1 is in M.
(b) If x is in M, then $y = 2 * x + 1$ and $z = 3 * x + 1$ are also in M.
(c) No other numbers are in M. $(M = \{1, 3, 4, 7, 9, 10 \dots\})$

15.13 Figure (15.73) shows a ring of 2^3 zeroes and ones in which each of the 2^3 possible sub-sequences of 3 binary digits occurs exactly once.

$\qquad$ (15.73)

Design an algorithm that generates such a ring, consisting of 2^n digits containing every possible sub-sequence of n digits exactly once. Follow the principle of stepwise program refinement.

15.14 Given is a $(n \times n)$ matrix R of relations. Construct an algorithm that computes natural numbers x_i and y_i $(i = 1, \dots, n)$ such that

(a) $x_i < y_i$, if $R_{ij} = $ less,
(b) $x_i = y_i$, if $R_{ij} = $ equal,
(c) $x_i > y_i$, if $R_{ij} = $ greater,

if such numbers exist, and otherwise assigns the value *false* to a Boolean variable q.

APPENDIX A
THE PROGRAMMING
LANGUAGE PASCAL†

BASIC SYMBOLS

$A \ldots Z, a \ldots z$	letters
0 1 2 3 4 5 6 7 8 9	digits
+ − * / **div mod**	arithmetic operators
∨ ∧ ¬	logical operators
= ≠ < ≦ ≧ > **in**	relational operators
( )	parentheses
[ ]	index brackets
{ }	comment braces
begin end	statement brackets
:=	assignment operator
'	quote mark
. , : ;	separators
↑	pointer symbol
if then else case of with	statement separators
while do repeat until for to	
const type var procedure function	object class specifiers
array file record set	structure class specifiers
nil	null pointer
goto label	jump operator, label declarator

STANDARD IDENTIFIERS

Constants:	*false, true*	(8.1)
Types:	*Boolean, integer, char, real, text*	(8.1–8.4)

† Revised version of definition in *Acta Informatica*, **1**, 35–63, (1971).

Variables:	*input, output*	(10.4)
Functions:	*abs, sqr, odd*	
	succ, pred	(8)
	ord, chr	(8.3)
	trunc, eof, eoln	(8.4, 10.3)
	sin, cos, exp, ln, sqrt, arctan	
Procedures:	*get, put, reset, rewrite*	(10.2–10.3)
	read, write, readln, writeln	(10.4)

OPERATORS

Relational operators (least priority):

=	≠			arbitrary operands, result *Boolean*	(8.3)
<	≦	≧	>	scalar operands, result *Boolean*	

Additive operators:

+	−	addition, subtraction	(8.2, 8.4)
∨		logical union (OR)	(8.1)

Multiplicative operators:

*	multiplication	(8.2, 8.4)
/	division, result *real*	(8.4)
div	division, result *integer*	(8.2)
mod	remainder of integer division	(8.2)
∧	logical disjunction (AND)	(8.1)

Monadic operator:

¬	logical negation (NOT)	(8.1)

STANDARD REPRESENTATION OF PASCAL PROGRAMS WITH THE RESTRICTED ASCII CHARACTER SET

1. Only capital letters are used.
2. No blanks may occur within identifiers, word delimiters, or numbers.
3. Basic symbols that are represented by English words [so-called *word delimiters*, are spelled out without surrounding escape characters. They cannot be used as identifiers, and if they are preceded or followed by another word delimiter or by an identifier, at least one blank character must occur in between.
4. PASCAL symbols not contained in the restricted ASCII set are translated as follows.

PASCAL Symbol			Corresponding ASCII Character(s)		
∨	∧	¬	OR	AND	NOT
≠	≦	≧	< >	<=	>=
{	}		(*	*)	

SYNTAX

IDENTIFIER

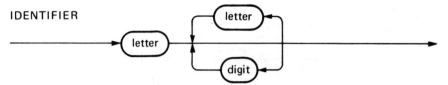

UNSIGNED INTEGER

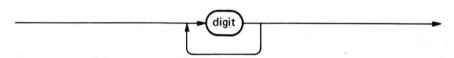

UNSIGNED NUMBER

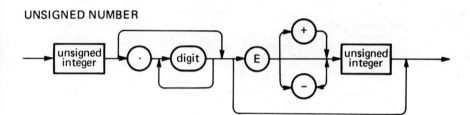

UNSIGNED CONSTANT

CONSTANT

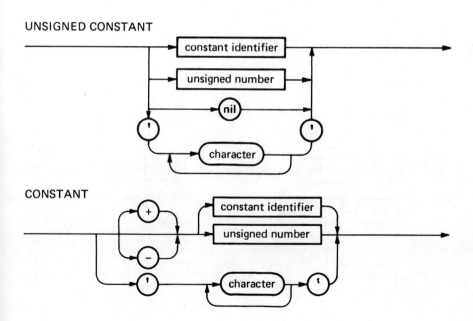

SIMPLE TYPE

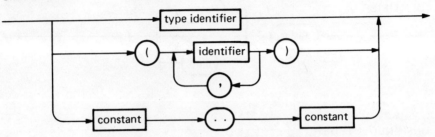

TYPE

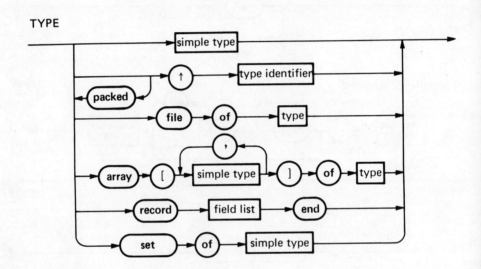

FIELD LIST

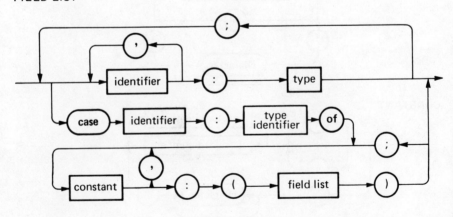

VARIABLE

FACTOR

TERM

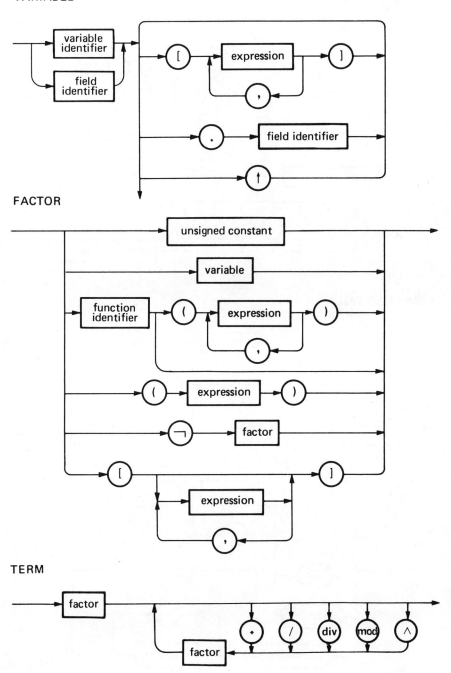

SIMPLE EXPRESSION

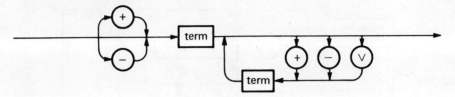

EXPRESSION

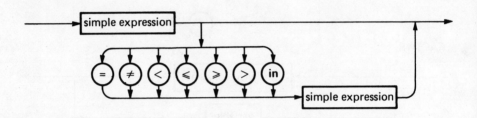

COMPOUND TAIL

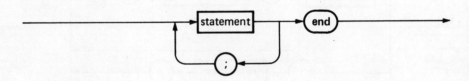

PARAMETER LIST

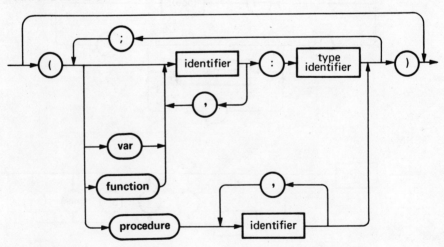

STATEMENT

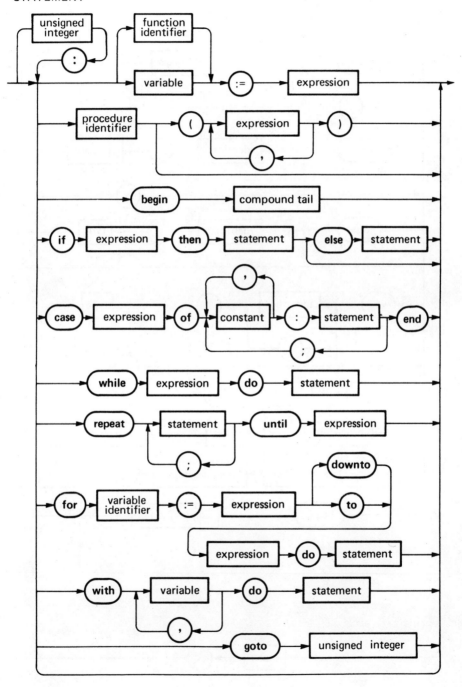

BLOCK

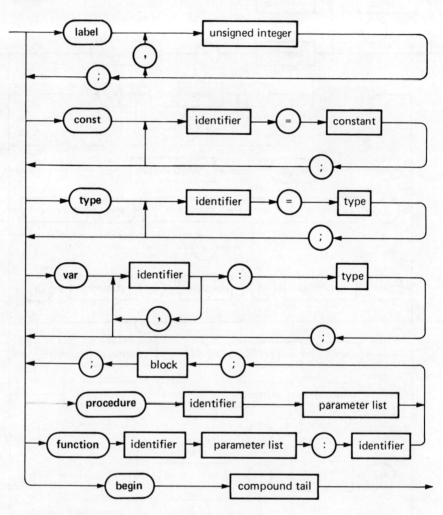

PROGRAM

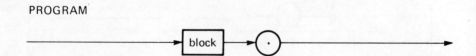

APPENDIX B
THE ASCII CHARACTER CODE

b_6	0	0	0	0	1	1	1	1
b_5	0	0	1	1	0	0	1	1
b_4	0	1	0	1	0	1	0	1
$b_3\text{–}b_0$								
0000	nul	dle		0	@	P	`	p
0001	soh	dc1	!	1	A	Q	a	q
0010	stx	dc2	"	2	B	R	b	r
0011	etx	dc3	#	3	C	S	c	s
0100	eot	dc4	$	4	D	T	d	t
0101	enq	nak	%	5	E	U	e	u
0110	ack	syn	&	6	F	V	f	v
0111	bel	etb	'	7	G	W	g	w
1000	bs	can	(	8	H	X	h	x
1001	ht	em	)	9	I	Y	i	y
1010	lf	sub	*	:	J	Z	j	z
1011	vt	esc	+	;	K	†[	k	†{
1100	ff	fs	,	<	L	\	l	|
1101	cr	gs	-	=	M	]	m	}
1110	so	rs	.	>	N	^	n	¬
1111	si	us	/	?	O	_	o	del

control characters   graphic characters

Restricted ASCII Character Set

† Undefined in the ISO Standard. Symbols vary among different national versions; this is the ASCII version.

163

THE MEANING OF CONTROL CHARACTERS
FOR DATA TRANSMISSION

REPRESENTATION ON PUNCHED PAPER TAPE

Layout characters:
bs   backspace
ht   horizontal tabulation
lf   line feed
vt   vertical tabulation
ff   form feed
cr   carriage return

Ignore characters:
nul   null characters
can   cancel
sub   substitute
del   delete

Separator characters:
fs   file separator
gs   group separator
rs   record separator
us   unit separator

Escape characters:
so   shift-out
si   shift-in
esc   escape

Medium control characters:
bel   ring bell
dc1–dc4   device control
em   end of medium

Communication control characters:
soh   start of heading
stx   start of text
etx   end of text
eot   end of transmission
enq   enquiry
ack   acknowledgment
nak   negative acknowledgment
dle   data link escape
syn   synchronous idle
etb   end of transmission block

SUBJECT INDEX

INDEX OF SAMPLE PROGRAMS